"For those of us who were n[...]
Monastic Institute in 2006, t[...]
useful. Anybody who is interested in the future of monasticism will find
these addresses and discussions quite fascinating. In this volume the
old monasticism meets the new."

— Terrence Kardong, OSB
Assumption Abbey
Richardton, North Dakota

"One Heart, One Soul: Many Communities captures a unique and lively
conversation between monastics rooted in the Benedictine tradition and
Christians from 'new monastic' and other intentional communities.
To read this volume is to engage in lively conversation about community
life with a variety of seasoned practitioners and teachers and those newer
to monasticism or intentional Christian community as they reflect on
the meaning and practices of their lives from various viewpoints of age,
experience, denomination, gender, and culture. The presentations, panels,
questions, and comments are informative, insightful, honest, and at times
passionate as they explore questions of spiritual meaning and daily
practice relative to traditional monastic values and their contemporary
expression: the common life and table, obedience and authority,
leadership, humility, discernment, and hospitality."

— Katherine Howard, OSB
St. Benedict's Monastery
St. Joseph, Minnesota

"One Heart, One Soul: Many Communities is the record of an early and
exciting stage of a conversation that is surely going to continue. The
dialogue partners are men and women, young and old, married and
celibate, Benedictine monastics, Benedictine oblates, Catholic Workers,
members of L'Arche, representatives of the 'New Monasticism,' and others
living in intentional Christian communities. St. Benedict says,
'Listen,' and there is much here that deserves a hearing. The Spirit
that set St. Benedict in motion is certainly at work in the twenty-first
century. In this well-edited collection of presentations and discussions
there are some strong hints of the directions that the divine Wind is
blowing today."

— Fr. Hugh Feiss, OSB
Monastery of the Ascension
Jerome, Idaho

One Heart, One Soul
Many Communities

Proceedings of the 21st Annual Monastic Institute
School of Theology-Seminary
Saint John's University
Collegeville, Minnesota 56321
July 1–7, 2006

Edited by Mary Forman, OSB

SAINT JOHN'S UNIVERSITY PRESS

COLLEGEVILLE, MINNESOTA

Cover design by Ann Blattner.

1   2   3   4   5   6   7   8   9

Library of Congress Cataloging-in-Publication Data

Monastic Institute (21st : 2006 : Saint John's University, Collegeville, Minn.)
   One heart, one soul, many communities : proceedings of the 21st Annual Monastic Institute, School of Theology-Seminary, Saint John's University, Collegeville, Minnesota 56321, July 1–7, 2006 / edited by Mary Forman.
      p. cm.
   "A Saint John's University Press book."
   Includes bibliographical references and index.
   ISBN 978-0-9740992-5-5 (pbk.)
   1. Benedictines—Congresses.   2. Monastic and religious life—Congresses.   I. Forman, Mary, 1947–   II. Title.
   BX3001.5.M66   2006
   255—dc22   2009001489

Contents

Preface

The summer of 1980 marked a major milestone for Benedictines worldwide as they celebrated the sesquimillennium of Saint Benedict with a two-week-long Monastic Institute from June 22 to July 4, 1980. Similarly, the summer of 2006 marked the sesquicentennial milestone for the Benedictine community at Saint John's Abbey and University. Memories of world-renowned speakers gathered for the Monastic Institute that summer of 1980 were in mind when the planning committee for the 21st Annual Monastic Institute met to gather ideas for theme, keynote speakers, and processes for the sesquicentennial Institute, to be held July 1–7, 2006.

Planners, keenly aware of the several forms of "new monasticism" that had sprung up within the last decades, as well as the seemingly downsizing of traditional forms of monastic communities in North America and Europe, felt the necessity to gather representatives of both groups to meet for an engaged conversation. Some 176 participants, speakers, and panelists gathered from all over the United States, from Rome, and Melbourne to engage in dialogue about new forms of intentional community, the need for continuing ecumenical efforts in order to build understanding across Christian traditions for living communal life more intently, and to explore values common to communities for authentic, truthful, vibrant Christian commitment. Each day featured a keynote speaker and a panel of responders or colloquium, followed by interaction with the participants who were eager to share observations, raise new questions, and offer critiques and/or support ideas. The talks are presented in this volume, along with a summary of the important dialogues that took place after sessions.

The talks and dialogue sessions capture only a part of this Institute, since many of the ongoing conversations were carried on by participants going to and from prayer, walks around campus, before and after three concerts, and in the hallways and during mealtimes. Key issues were raised at sessions, which only reinforced the need for ongoing dialogue; such topics included the following: Where are the women at the altar? How does obedience differ for monastics and married people with families? How do individualism and technology pose problems for communal living and for being aware of the common good? In what ways is there a need for discernment when truth telling is called for in communities of broken people? How do leadership and members deal with members of community who have decidedly excommunicated themselves from the community? How do the diverse cultures that can exist in a given community—intergenerations, ethnicities, orientations, ecumenical—both enrich and challenge the day-to-day life in community? The final session closed with an invitation to traditional Benedictine communities: How might they extend their wisdom regarding formation, intergenerational living, and structures for communal living to the new communities? In turn, how might the new communities offer new hope, vibrancy, and venues for the Spirit to do something "new" to the traditional communities?

Deep gratitude is expressed to the members of the planning committee for the 2006 Monastic Institute: Bill Cahoy; William Skudlarek, OSB; Colleen Haggerty, OSB; Don Ottenhoff; Linda Schreiber; and Vic Klimoski. Thanks to a generous grant from the Louisville Institute several participants were able to come to this gathering and share their wisdom. Special thanks go to Linda Schreiber and Kristi Bivens for their assistance in all the details for the Institute.

Mary Forman, OSB

Abbreviations

ABECA   Benedictine Association of the Caribbean and Andes

AIM   Alliance for International Monasticism

BECOSA   Benedictine Communities of Southern Africa

CIB   Communion Internationalis Benedictinarum

DIM   Dialogue Interreligieux Monastique

EMLA   Encuentro Monastico Latino Americano

Heb   Hebrews`

OSB   Order of Saint Benedict

OSCO   Order of Cistercians of the Strict Observance

PIL   Pontifical Institute of Liturgy

RB   Rule of Benedict

SGS   Sisters of the Good Samaritan

Zech   Zechariah

Section I

Global Setting of Monasticism

"Community movements today . . . may parse the concept of community differently from the classic monastic model; they try to find ways to strive for genuine interdependence while not excluding some autonomy; they may work out ways of accountability within a range of participation: temporary/permanent; live-in/live-out; no vows/vowed/covenanted; married/celibate; leader/consensus model. While classic monasticism relies on a permanent identification with a particular community, which is described in the Benedictine concept of stability, there are other approaches today in which the identification becomes occasional, more a kind of reference point, or even a place of return for reconnection."

— Columba Stewart, OSB

Early Monasticism and Community Movements Today

What Is Old and New and How Do They Meet?

Columba Stewart, OSB[1]

It is a great pleasure to be here this evening and to see what is surely the largest gathering ever of people for the Monastic Institute. My purpose is to start a conversation that will continue in various arenas, formal and informal, over the course of the Institute, by addressing the topic: "Early Monasticism and Community Movements Today: What Is Old and New and How Do They Meet?"

Now I will admit in all humility that I think I know a fair amount about early monasticism. But to paraphrase a classic of American film, "I don't know nothing about birthing 'new community movements.'" I am, however, a product of the same culture as those who have been instrumental in these movements; I know what it is like to live in community in the twenty-first century, and I have spent a significant part of the past years working with people, young men

---

1. Columba Stewart, OSB, monk of Saint John's Abbey, Collegeville, Minnesota, is the executive director of the Hill Museum and Manuscript Library and University Vice-President for Programs in Religion and Culture, Saint John's University. He is the author of *"Working the Earth of the Heart": The Messalian Controversy in History, Texts, and Language to A.D. 431*, Oxford Theological Monographs (Oxford, 1991); *The World of the Desert Fathers: Stories and Sayings from the Anonymous Series of the Apophthegmata Patrum* (Fairacres, 1997); *Prayer and Community: The Benedictine Tradition*, Traditions of Christian Spirituality (Orbis, 1998); and *Cassian the Monk*, Oxford Studies in Historical Theology (Oxford, 1999).

and women, who have been discerning a call to monastic life, to marriage, or to other major commitments. So, the resulting observations, which I will share with you this evening, will be historical, personal, social, and best of all, anecdotal.

Early Monasticism

First, I will offer what will be the heaviest and most academic part of my reflections with some comments about **early monasticism**. So, we start with the heavy stuff, and then ease off as we move more into the modern age. At the outset, early monasticism is a phenomenon even more complex than the variety of new community movements that we can find today, varying in language, culture, geography, understanding of the life and relationship to the local church, and so on. So, we need to situate monasticism in its historical context.

Despite our best efforts as Christian monastics today to search for biblical origins of who we are and what we do, we need to admit that Christians did not invent the notion of what today we call "intentional community." In the late antique world in which Christianity took root, there were numerous forms of ideologically based association. There were philosophical fellowships of various kinds, which survived well into the Christian Era (Pythagoreans). In Palestinian Judaism at the time of Jesus there were the Essenes and the Qumran community associated with the Dead Sea Scrolls. Jesus' own Galilean fellowship with its core group of disciples fit a familiar pattern of radical commitment to a charismatic teacher, as did John the Baptist's perhaps rival group in the Judean desert near the River Jordan. Ascetics in the Mesopotamian heartland of the Syriac Christians made commitments to celibate membership in covenantal communities as early as the third and fourth centuries and maybe even before that. Egypt, home of the earliest famous Christian "monastic" experiments, had also been the location for Philo's mysterious "Therapeutae," an esoteric Jewish sect in the environs of Alexandria that Philo claimed was to be found in many other regions. Indeed, you might say that Egypt was the great spiritual theme park of the ancient world, where what we would call from our historical perspective "orthodox" or "catholic" Christians (in other words, those viewed from later perspective as mainstream and rooted in what became the canonical Scriptures) rubbed elbows constantly with a dozen flavors of Gnosticism and other late antique "New Age" movements. All of this took place against the dramatic backdrop of the vast desert and the great monuments of the ancient Egyptian cults.

The Search for Monastic Origins

What then was "early monasticism" that is used as a reference point for looking at community movements today? The search for monastic origins has been a significant concern of post-Reformation and post-Enlightenment scholarship. Its myriad results have made this search analogous to the better-known effort to locate the Jesus of history. The search for monastic origins may perhaps have been more successful than the search for the historical Jesus; nonetheless, its protagonists have not by any means avoided the pitfall ascribed to Adolf von Harnack, greatest of modern historians, by the Catholic modernist George Tyrrell. Writing in 1909 of Harnack's portrait of Jesus, Tyrrell states, "The Christ that Harnack sees, looking back through nineteen centuries of Catholic darkness, is only the reflection of a Liberal Protestant face, seen at the bottom of a deep well."[2] The face that Harnack saw, of course, was his own. As we look at studies of early monasticism from the Reformation period to Edward Gibbon to the most recent scholarship, we find "explanations" for monasticism ranging from flight to the desert to avoid conscription or taxes, to voluntary self-sacrifice in a world in which martyrdom had become démodé, or the appearance of a new and particularly nasty form of "the virus of asceticism";[3] some have characterized

2. George Tyrrell, "The Christ of Liberal Protestantism," in *Christianity at the Crossroads* (London/New York: Longmans, Green and Co., 1909), 49.

3. Norman Douglas, "Southern Saintliness," in *Old Calabria*, rev. ed. (London: Gentry Books/Century Printing, 1915; repr. 1983), 251. See also Norman Douglas, "*Old Calabria* on Authorama: Public Domain Books" at the following web site: http://www.authorama.com/old-calabria-31.html.

monasticism as a takeover by pro-Nicene episcopal thought-police of a formerly independent-minded asceticism that had empowered both men and women. Despite whatever reason is adduced and is so often the case, the truth is probably a compounding of all these various glimpses, the phenomenon itself was extraordinary: as Gibbon, the finest, if at times the most offensive, writer among the early explainers, wrote: "The Egyptians . . . were disposed to hope, and to believe, that the number of monks was equal to the remainder of the people; and posterity might repeat the saying [in the Christian era], which had formerly been applied to the sacred animals of the same country, that, in Egypt, it was less difficult to find a god than a man."[4] So, historians hoped that the same would be said of monastic men and women. You read the early statistic that one diocese had ten thousand monks and as always twice as many nuns.[5] You find similar statistics reflecting this extraordinary explosion of what people were suddenly calling monasticism at the end of the third and beginning of the fourth centuries.

The Development of Early Monasticism and Later Transformations

I have my own way of understanding this sudden irruption of monasticism into the Roman world, and one that I hope avoids Harnack's narcissistic well or an overly simple analysis of what is, after all, a highly complex phenomenon. It goes like this. In the late third and early fourth centuries certain individuals and their followers began to emerge from a kind of primordial ascetic soup in Egypt and Asia Minor. By this point they have attained a stage of self-conscious identity or organizational development that suddenly makes them particularly noticeable, with practices that seem "more than" the

---

4. Edward Gibbon, *The Decline and Fall of the Roman Empire*, Great Books of the Western World, ed. Mortimer J. Adler, 2nd ed. (Chicago, IL: Encyclopaedia Britannica, 1990): 1:594, chap. 37, col. 2.

5. *The Lives of the Desert Fathers: the Historia Monachorum in Aegypto*, trans. Norman Russell, Cistercian Studies 48 (London & Oxford: Mowbray/Kalamazoo, MI: Cistercian Publications, 1980), 67, with reference to "Oxyrynchus, one of the cities of the Thebaid."

Christian or even ascetic norm. They have begun to establish traditions of teaching and distinctive terminology. Sometimes, as was the case of Egypt, given the unique geography of the river running through the land and desert readily accessible, footsteps away from the fertile strip along the river, these people seemed to exhibit a preference for physically isolated locations that made them all the easier to recognize, and indeed for seekers, all the easier to find. They also began to benefit from episcopal patronage: Antony of Egypt most famously got Athanasius of Alexandria as his postmortem publicist, for better or worse, in terms of the actual historicity of some details of Antony's life. Basil the Great took over and established ascetic communities in Cappadocia and Asia Minor. The individual circumstances of each one of these great figures, or of each regional experiment (I call them experiments because most of them did not last very long for all kinds of reasons), are distinctive and resistant to uniform etiology. One might, finally, have to allow that we believers do find, after we have played every other card in our hand, that the Holy Spirit might have had something to do with all of it.

It is fair to say, and this is crediting some of the work of the great scholars of the period, that in the early Christian period and in later centuries, monasticism and other great religious "movements" flourished in times of social transition or transformation, whether in sympathetic response to whatever was happening in that transition or transformation or as a kind of manifest reaction to what was happening. For all kinds of reasons the fourth through seventh centuries were certainly stressful, opening with the end of persecution, and soon became enmeshed in exhausting doctrinal debates that became genuinely church dividing (the effects of which we live with today in many of the regions, where our work with manuscripts tries to heal divisions that date to the fourth and fifth centuries). The same period saw the fall of the Western empire, which was devastating psychologically for Western Christians and others, and ended with a tremendous catastrophe—the rise of Islam and the loss of much of the Christian East to the new faith. The ninth century, when Benedictine monasticism finally made it big through imperial patronage, was a period of reconsolidation after all of that had happened. The twelfth century saw the rise of cities and universities, and a breakout from the classic monastic pattern, as the so-called new orders responded to social and religious needs in ways that traditional monasticism simply could not, and as monasticism itself was essentially refounded through several kinds of reform. The sixteenth-century Reformation and Counter-Reformation was certainly another time of transformation and monastic response. The nineteenth century was one of change, with its revolutionary closure of monasteries and their refounding in different forms, some of which looked either backward to a romanticized, traditionally ordered world, or some of which absorbed the principle of social utility and engaged in new forms of educational and pastoral mission. That latter kind of monasticism brought us to this place.

Many people would argue that ours is such a transitional or transformational period, shifting from Euro-American hegemony to a much more complicated global politics. Within the Euro-American world the last fifty years have seen the collapse of former assumptions about authority, morality, and the place of the church. Ideologically driven mass movements of the twentieth century such as Communism and Fascism may now seem remote from Western countries, but it is only fair to say that the polarized political atmosphere and culture wars in the United States and the increase of religious and ethnic intolerance everywhere else do not encourage ease. Meanwhile, say scientists, the whole planet has become the frog in that famous experiment, unaware that it is slowly being boiled alive as we suffer through global warming.

In light of all this, how could classic monasticism *not* be in for quite a ride in the decades to come? And how could there *not* be some really interesting things happening outside the historical monastic movements?

Reasons Proposed for Why Early Christians Joined Monastic Movements

To help us understand some of what may have been going on both inside and outside classic monasticism today in this time, I propose that we start by examining some of the reasons why early Christians might have joined monastic movements, and then compare some of their motivations for exploring monastic or other communities expressed by people today. This will be very sketchy, but may provide something of a catalyst to our further reflection and discussion.

Why did late antique, or early Christian, men and women join monasteries? As always, because I have some historical training, I have to issue a disclaimer about the nature of the evidence. The evidence is written; it is not live. We do not have oral histories of these early monastic figures. The literature was rarely first person, and it was often spun by what we call in the scholarly world hagiographers and what are called today in the corporate world spinmasters. Nonetheless, the historical record that we can find in these monastic texts can serve as "typical": both in terms of expressing some of the common motivations, perhaps more dramatically than was typically the case, and also "typical" in the sense of being formative or inspirational for others in their interest in and approach to monastic life.

Repentance

When you consult the sources, the number one motivation that you find was one that sounds highly antique to us: **repentance**. If we call the word "conversion," or even better use words like *metanoia*, it becomes more palatable to us, but our early monastic forebears were not hesitant to use the great "R" word. The working assumption, which after all is the working assumption of the anthropology of the Rule of Benedict, was that we are indeed screwed-up people who need a way to get back on track. This explains the appeal of John the Baptist in early monasticism as a great monastic type among the Old Testament and New Testament figures: after all, "Repent" was his great sound bite. As a result, monastic literature, early and medieval, and in any case premodern, is full of dramatic stories of repentance and conversion. We all know Augustine's account in the *Confessions*, which led him to a celibate life in community. But there were other figures who perhaps may be more intriguing, because they are less familiar or more attractive, because we have less baggage of our own when we consider them. One of these is Moses the Ethiopian,[6] a brigand and murderer moved to repentance by meeting the gentle monastic inhabitants of the salt marshes of Scetis, as he hid out in the Egyptian desert. He then follows their example, becoming a monk and a great teacher. Later in life he finds himself attacked by marauding Bedouin, the sort of people he once was; as they devastated his adopted monastic home, he offered them no resistance, having begun as a brigand and murderer and dying as a martyr of nonviolence. In another vein, Sister Benedicta Ward has written about the many stories of prostitutes who escaped a life of sexual slavery and found healing and wholeness in monastic life.[7] Among them were figures like Mary of Egypt and Pelagia, who became types of monastic repentance and whose stories translated into Latin became staples of medieval general Christian instruction. These dramatic examples must not obscure the undramatic thousands for whom life had lost its freshness, or who had become weary of their burden of sinfulness and who longed for a new beginning. In the twentieth century, one need look no further than Thomas Merton, who tapped into this same vein as they told their stories. One wonders if such a tale as Merton's would sell today.

Social Relocation

Second among early Christian reasons for being interested in monasticism, there was a desire for **social relocation**; that sounds scientific and appropriately objective. The term—desire for social relocation—works because ancient peoples were locked into places and relationships in a way that we can scarcely imagine. Village and family defined the boundaries of one's existence, and everyone had a

6. "Moses," in *The Sayings of the Desert Fathers: The Alphabetical Collection*, trans. Benedicta Ward, Cistercian Studies 59, 138–43 (London & Oxford: Mowbray/ Kalamazoo, MI: Cistercian Publications, 1975).

7. Benedicta Ward, *Harlots of the Desert: A Study of Repentance in Early Monastic Sources*, Cistercian Studies 106 (Kalamazoo, MI: Cistercian Publications, 1987).

role to play that was inexorably determined by social class, gender, and birth order. Some of the most famous early monks fled this burden of expectation. For example, Antony the Great, with the sudden death of his parents, found himself a person of importance in his village, owner of a substantial amount of land and guardian of his younger sister. As one hears the story of his call to "sell everything and follow me" and "do not worry about tomorrow,"[8] it is hard to escape the suspicion that, for Antony, taking his Daddy's place at the grain exchange and the coffee shop was more than he could bear. Equally, Gregory's depiction of the young Benedict scandalized by the adolescent experiments of his peers in Rome and running away from boarding school (accompanied by his devoted nanny) suggests something of the same reluctance or constitutional inability to follow a path that was predetermined for him by others. Numerous modern scholars have been particularly interested in the extraordinary courage of early ascetic and monastic women, who followed their own preference for asceticism rather than their parents' expectation of advantageous marriage and traditional motherhood. In a world that was even more restrictive than the nun-nurse-teacher-librarian or marriage world of not so long ago, asceticism was a real breakout opportunity for women, especially for those who lacked personal wealth and the independence that wealth could buy. Many of the famous women of the Latin monastic world especially, who became patrons of monastic men like Jerome and Rufinus and others, were wealthy widows whose choice to pursue their own distinctive monastic vocation was made possible by the allowance of female property-holding under Roman law. For others, wealth could not buy their freedom, but gradually as monasticism took hold it became an option.

There were other kinds of social relocation that early monasticism offered, such as *xeniteia*, that is, voluntary exile from one's native country, which was a harsh asceticism to be perpetually a stranger, as well as fosterage, the placement of unwanted or unaffordable children in monasteries. I noted with interest that the web

---

8. Athanasius, *The Life of St. Antony*, trans. Robert T. Meyer, Ancient Christian Writers 10 (New York/Ramsey, NJ: Newman Press, 1978), chaps. 2–3, 19–20.

site of the New Monasticism project presents as one of the twelve marks of the movement, "relocation to the abandoned places of Empire."[9] This was after I came up with this phrase of "social relocation."

Fulfillment of a Vow

The third reason for undertaking monasticism in the early period was doing so as **fulfillment of a vow**. Pachomius related that he became a Christian and village ascetic because of a vow he made at a time of crisis. Having been conscripted by the Romans in the particularly violent way they did conscription in those days, which was to go into a village, ask to see all the young men between certain ages, put them in chains and shackles, haul them far from home, drop them on a battlefield, and then say, "Fight your way out." Pachomius, finding himself in such a situation, also had his first encounter with Christians and, in some desperation, as people often do, tried praying to their God for deliverance to see if that would work, having tried his own.[10] Sure enough, it worked, and off he went: baptism, asceticism, and then a career as a monastic experimenter, with mixed success until he finally got the formula right, about which more will be said later. Evagrius Ponticus abandoned a very promising ecclesiastical career in Constantinople after having promised in a dream that he would break off a dalliance with a rich married lady and get out of town fast.[11] Theodoret of Cyrrhus, author of a famous series of literary vignettes of Syrian monks of the fifth cen-

---

9. *School(s) for Conversion: 12 Marks of a New Monasticism*, ed. Rutba House (Eugene, OR: Cascade Books, a Division of Wipf & Stock Publishers, 2005), xii, where this phrase is listed as the first mark of a new monasticism. See also http://www.newmonasticism.org/12marks/index.html.

10. "The Bohairic Life of Pachomius 7–8," in *Pachomian Koinonia I: The Life of Saint Pachomius and His Disciples*, trans. Armand Veilleux, Cistercian Studies 45 (Kalamazoo, MI: Cistercian Publications, 1980), 26–28. See also the parallel to this story in the same volume, "The First Greek Life of Pachomius 4–5," 300–301.

11. See "38. Evagrius," in *Palladius: The Lausiac History*, trans. Robert T. Meyer, Ancient Christian Writers 34 (New York/Mahwah, NJ: Paulist Press, 1964), 110–14.

tury, was promised to the church by his mother even before his conception, and his birth was attributed to the prayers of a monk who was a friend of the family.[12] All this can seem strange to us, but as we talk to people who come from traditional Catholic families, many of them in this room, and as I hear people tell stories of what it was like in this part of the country not so long ago, such a world is not so very distant from our own time.

Fulfillment of a Spiritual Aspiration

Finally, there was monasticism as the **fulfillment of spiritual aspiration or a desire for advancement**. The young John Cassian longed to be a "soldier of Christ"[13] rather than of the emperor, a kind of male analogue to the young woman who preferred betrothal to Christ to marriage to an earthly groom. Where else did talented overachievers in the late antique Christian world direct their energy? Monasticism was the coming thing. Had the young Benjamin Braddock in Mike Nichol's brilliant film *The Graduate* (1967) lived in the year 450 rather than in the 1960s, the sage word of advice offered to him at his graduation party would not have been "Plastics" but "Monasticism." Over time in the history of the church this became only truer, as monasticism offered the talented men and women an opportunity for advancement that a very tightly structured society could not itself offer.

Proposed Reasons Men and Women Join Monasteries Today

So, with that background let me venture tentatively some observations about:

---

12. "Macedonius XIII.16-18," in Theodoret of Cyrrhus, *A History of the Monks of Syria*, trans. R. M. Price, Cistercian Studies 88 (Kalamazoo, MI: Cistercian Publications, 1985), 105–7.

13. There are several references to *miles Christi* or "soldier of Christ" in Cassian's Institutes; see *John Cassian: The Institutes*, trans. Boniface Ramsey, Ancient Christian Writers 58 (New York/Mahwah, NJ: Newman Press, 2000): *Inst.* I.1.1, 21; II.1, 37; V.19.1, 129; V.21.1, 130; VII.21, 180; X.3, 220-21; XI.3, 241; and XI.7, 243.

Why do (post-) modern men and women join monasteries or get interested in various community movements? I can speak here only of men and women in North America and western Europe—the culture that I know. In other parts of the world, many of these reasons of what I mentioned above are still very much in play, along with cultural and local variance of the same.

#1: *Desire for Community*

Surely the primary reason that we all hear is the **desire for community**. Having experienced the social fragmentation of the postindustrial world, many people have a longing for social integration. In a world in which "online community" is not an oxymoron, this surely cannot be surprising. People want connection with others, and just as important, they want that connection with others to be healthy. There are a lot of unhealthy options out there for connecting with others. Intentional communities, monastic or otherwise, can offer places of genuine humanity, shared commitments, and relational sanity. In preparation for this talk I spoke with several young people who have considered monastic life. Each one mentioned as his or her first reason for considering monastic life "support" and over the long haul, as the most attractive aspect of monastic community. Recent social surveys consider that the average American had now gone from three trusted friends to two. This has prompted a lot of reflection among sociologists of "the bowling alone variety,"[14] who have looked at the corrosion of the traditional forms of civic association in our country. Whatever the validity of statistics like this, it is striking that there are plenty of people who would say that they have no trusted other, which would allow for that statistical result of the norm being two.

Mark Epstein, a New York–based Buddhist psychotherapist, probes the roots of this modern longing in his book *Thoughts without a Thinker*. This guy has great marketing with books with titles like

---

14. See Robert D. Putnam, *Bowling alone: the collapse and revival of American community* (New York: Simon & Schuster, 2000).

Thoughts without a Thinker, Going to Pieces without Falling Apart, and his newer one, *Going on Being;* this is really terrific branding. In *Thoughts without a Thinker,* he contrasts what he has discovered about Tibetan culture with what he knows all too well from his practice about modern American culture:

> The eastern self is enmeshed in a web of family, hierarchy, caste, or other group expectations from which the only escape is often spiritual practice. . . . An ancient Buddhist text begins, "This generation is entangled in a tangle." . . . The starting point in the West rarely is an enmeshed self; more commonly it is an estranged one. The emphasis on individuality and autonomy, the breakdown of the extended and even the nuclear family, the scarcity of "good enough" parenting, and the relentless drive for achievement versus affection in our society leave a person all too often feeling cut off, isolated, alienated, empty, and longing for an intimacy that seems both out of reach and vaguely threatening.[15]

Epstein goes on to describe a meeting between Eastern spiritual masters and Western therapists sponsored by His Holiness the Dalai Lama: "The Dalai Lama was incredulous at the notion of 'low self-esteem' that he kept hearing about [from the Western participants]. He went around the room asking each Westerner there, 'Do you have this? Do you have this?' When they all nodded yes, he just shook his head in disbelief."[16] The Tibetan experience for those raised in that traditional Eastern milieu, like the Dalai Lama and other masters in that dialogue, was the world of our monastic ancestors, a world in which one came to a monastery to discover solitude for the first time in one's life, to wrestle with it, to find an individual identity, to shake up a reflexive self-confidence, and thus perhaps all Saint Benedict's warnings about self-will and his emphasis on a humility that to many modern readers seems unhealthy because our starting point is often so different from his. That was a world in which excommunication from community exercises really worked as punishment, rather than

---

15. Mark Epstein, *Thoughts without a Thinker: Psychotherapy from a Buddhist Perspective* (New York: Basic Books, a Division of HarperCollins, 1995), 176–77.
16. Ibid., 177.

in our world in which alienated individualism itself is the pathology that monastic life means to address.

This premier desire expressed by modern people for community begs the question, **what kind of community?** This is one of the major topics of our Institute this year. The classic monastic model is clear: it means a vowed, celibate, common life; community of goods; accountability shaped by obedience to a Rule and a superior; and that myriad of monastic customs that constitutes the framework for monastic life in a particular place. The great "ah-ha!" moment of cenobitic evolution came when Pachomius, living out the vow he had made as he lay in prison figuring out how to get out of the Roman army, realized that he couldn't achieve his hoped-for goal for *koinonia*, a community, without requiring that material goods be commonly owned and expectations be commonly understood.[17] His earlier experiment, where he thought he would live like a nice guy, and others would notice and start to imitate, and one day it would be the early Jerusalem, was a disaster.[18] Community movements today, including those that are expressed in this Institute, may parse the concept of community differently from the classic monastic model; they try to find ways to strive for genuine interdependence while not excluding some autonomy; they may work out ways of accountability within a range of participation: temporary/permanent; live-in/live-out; no vows/vowed/covenanted; married/celibate; leader/consensus model. While classic monasticism relies on a permanent identification with a particular community, which is described in the Benedictine concept of stability, there are other approaches today in which the identification becomes occasional, more a kind of reference point, or even a place of return for reconnection.

17. See "The Bohairic Life of Pachomius 23–26," in *Pachomian Koinonia I: The Life of Saint Pachomius and His Disciples*, 45–49; the parallel in this same volume appears as "The First Greek Life of Pachomius 24–28," 312–16.

18. See especially, "The Sahidic Life of Pachomius: Fragment IV," in *Pachomian Koinonia I*, 436–38.

#2: *Desire for a Life with Meaning and Purpose*

The second reason is the **desire for a life with meaning and purpose**. Many of us who have joined monasteries have done so from a desire, strong but often vague, for "something more" than we found in professional life or in the dating game. Many people today, celibate or married, have found themselves increasingly aware of the hollowness of much that passes for "life," have had experiences that caused them to glimpse the contingency of human existence evoked so powerfully in the book of Ecclesiastes, a monastic favorite. They quit their successful careers to pursue something with more "meaning" even at great financial and personal cost. Meanwhile, Corporate America is scrambling to catch up, to attend to concerns about quality of life, about balance between work and personal life in a 24/7 world, lest they lose their best-performing workers to something as horrific as the nonprofit sector. The "something more" so many of us seek is beyond my ability to characterize in this talk, for it is highly personal and deeply spiritual. It leads to my third and final reason.

#3: *Desire for a Structured, Substantial, Spiritual Life*

The third reason is the **desire for a structured, substantial, spiritual life**. The biggest growth area in publishing today, as many of us know, is in spirituality and religion. The Christian market is huge. One's local Barnes and Noble or Borders bookshop would make even the late antique Alexandrian Hellenist envious with the array of life paths that are on offer. While many of them will lead to the false gods of "self-fulfillment" or "success," many of them testify to the tremendous longing for something transcendent and substantial. In the third century, Origen of Alexandria and, later, of Caesarea in Palestine, deliberately addressed the yuppies of his day with writings of depth, intelligence, and serious engagement with the questions and thought-world of their time. The fascination that we find today with spiritualities seems somehow "authentic," whether they be practices from Asian religions, Sufi traditions, or the Christian East, is a stunning feature of the religious marketplace. How many American Roman Catholics or Protestants fifty years ago were reading books about praying with icons? Who could have guessed that a bookstore in Saint Cloud, Minnesota, would sell dozens of titles on Buddhist religious practice? Who could have predicted the interest in meditation in its various Buddhist, Hindu, or Christian forms? Who would have thought that even traditional Catholic practices, like Perpetual Adoration, would be revived as a mark of parish renewal?

When I look back at my arrival at Saint John's at the very beginning of the 1980s, the oblate program seemed to be on its last legs. It in no way registered on the screen of our common life or sense of mission. At the time, other religious orders seemed to have the retreat business sewn up. What happened? Whence this guesthouse building across the way, and others like it? Surely this growing desire for connection to a spiritual path that is structured and substantial is at least part of the explanation for what has happened. *Lectio divina*, the Psalms, books on monastic spirituality that focus not on dramatic stories of conversion but on the value of a spirituality grounded in Scripture and regular participation in the Liturgy of the Hours and Eucharist, laypeople applying the Rule of Benedict to family life, the legal profession, corporate world: who would have thought?

Conclusion

And so this leads me to conclude, not with Antony the Great, or Adolf von Harnack, Gibbon, or even Benedict, but with the one "who has spoken through the Prophets" (cf. Hosea 12:10; Zech 7:12), the Holy Spirit who is the only possible explanation for this gathering on a summer evening at a monastery far removed from Egypt, from Monte Cassino, from Bavaria. How else could I, a native of Houston, be delivered from my native Texanity to be brought to this land of "Minnesota-nice"? The Spirit, whom we profess has spoken through the Prophets, has given a message not about individual perfection but about the renewal of community. The message is always addressed to the people of Israel. In these coming days, let us listen, keenly, expectantly, and prayerfully, for a Spirit who seems to prefer whispers to trumpets, who calls each one of us to the renewal of our lives in loving communion with one another.

Dialogue with Columba Stewart, OSB

Would you say that the three reasons you gave for the present interest in monasticism—desire for community, for meaning and purpose, and a structured spiritual life—also explain what draws oblates to communities?

Columba: It is always interesting to hear one's own tradition refracted back, especially when oblates speak about Benedictine monasticism. One of the things that has happened to us in the last twenty-something years since the movement has found new legs is that it has challenged us to understand the tradition better and to be grateful for what we have.

William Skudlarek: Some time ago, and I only have very limited information on this, someone suggested to me that one of the reasons monasticism sprang up the way it did in Egypt was because of Christians being fascinated by some Buddhist missionary monks from India. There seems to be some evidence for some kind of Buddhist synod held in Alexandria, and that, in fact, Christians who imitated these Buddhist ascetics, who were referred to as the *gymnoi*, "the naked ones," were criticized. They were told that this was not an appropriate way of following the Christian life. I continue to be fascinated by the fact that this monastic phenomenon is one that predates Christianity, as you indicated in the area of Middle Eastern Greece, and five hundred years before it arose in Egypt. It has a universal character to it. I just wonder to what degree you might have some observations on whether that Christian brand of monasticism was in fact influenced from a much earlier strand, and if in some way that might be part of the reason for the renewed interest in other forms of monasticism today as expressed in Monastic Interreligious Dialogue?

Columba: One of the interesting things that has happened in modern scholarship is the willingness for people like me, who do monastic history from inside the movement, to be less defensive about parallels and sources and to recognize, for example, that much of the early desert understanding of the passions and the thoughts active in the human person are certainly derived from what Stoic philosophers and analysts had been reflecting on. What that shows is the openness of Christianity and the great tradition to engage seriously the cultures that are around it. We certainly see the same thing happening today. In terms of the direct connection between Buddhist monasticism and Christian monasticism, a lot of people have talked about the parallels, but I have not yet seen the missing-link evidence. There are indications that in the ancient world, despite what I said about your village defining your world and so on, people traveled a lot more than we would credit them, even though travel was arduous. Just think of the traffic up and down the silk road over the centuries. Early Syriac Christianity understands the mission of the biblical figure they associate with their founding, which is an amalgam of the apostle they call Judas Thomas. They mention a missionary trip he took to India, which has become a big part of the understanding of Indian Christians about the origin of their Christianity. What this tells us is that there were things going on along those trade routes that will always remain inaccessible to us. Our best stance is to learn what we can from the evidence available and not to be defensive, because, after all, our authenticity as Christian monastics does not rest on the framework of practices of monasticism; it rests on the religious faith that underlies that, which we express in these particular forms, which do begin to look like an archetype across the great traditions. The same can be said of Islam. So, many of the distinctive, devotional practices of Islam are clearly based on Christian practice, and I would say particularly monastic practice, not only in the Sufi traditions, but generally speaking: prostrations, Ramadan in Lent, and so on. That is just a fact of human culture.

Jonathan Wilson-Hartgrove: I am here as a representative of the New Monasticism. Just this past weekend I was in the hills of east Tennessee where we had a gathering of folks who were interested in community or starting new communities to get together and talk. Five hundred people showed up out of nowhere. As we talked together, all three things you mentioned were very much there: this longing for community, longing for connection, and for a sense of purpose. But a few of us for the past year have been trying to read the Rule of Saint Benedict seriously and to see how the three vows inform what we are doing. The one I was most struck by was obedience and the sense that while the longing among this group of mostly young people is very genuine, exactly what are we obedient to? Obedience, more than anything, is offensive to our sort of American self-expression. Could you say something of where people, who are coming at this from unconventional trails, can look for obedience or a model of what that could look like?

Columba: If you want to hear about monastic obedience, you should really have a prioress or abbot speak to you. The prominence of obedience in the classic monastic tradition points to the fact that finding ways to pull people out of themselves and to connect them to this something larger has been a perennial challenge. It certainly is a concept that is offensive to my personal self-expression, so this is a challenge within monastic movements themselves. In terms of where you might look—marriage, children, commitment to communities—there is a lot more obedience, and certainly there is a lot more asceticism out there in American culture than we realize. Not all of it is healthy. You know we diet for beauty sometimes rather than for health or for God. But there is a lot that is healthy, and teasing out some elements of that could be really beneficial. I find my greatest lesson is in watching my married sisters and my friends who are married with small children. I am in awe of that kind of obedience, because that is not optional, not when you have the kids.

Catholic Worker: I have been with the Catholic Worker Movement for a long time. For the people who are gathered to the Worker, I am amazed that there seems to be an agreement that we live at the end of the empire; we live in a society that is non-sustainable; it's ready to fall apart and it should fall apart. Dorothy Day said, "All our problems stem from our acceptance of a filthy, rotten system." We look to the Benedictines and to the Desert Fathers and Mothers living in times very similar to ours, when all the institutions they depended on and trusted, their whole society, was on the verge of collapse. And how do you live? My friends at a Catholic Worker Farm in South Dakota say that they are practicing for when peace breaks out, because when the people of the world are allowed to use the land the way they choose and use labor to feed themselves and their own families, instead of supporting us, they are going to be using it very differently. We are going to have to figure out: How will we feed ourselves? How will we house ourselves? How will we keep warm in the winter when we will not have these things to depend on? What we'll have to depend on is community. We have a society now that makes it very, very difficult to love. We need to build something very different, as things are falling apart around us; we build an alternative.

Columba: I was trying not to get too apocalyptic in my own evocation of the post-Euro-American hegemony, but it is difficult not to have the sense that between the political and religious currents in the world and the unsustainability of our dependence on petroleum, there is something pretty big around the corner. The arguments among the people who study this seem to be more about "when" as opposed to "if." So, then the question of intentional communities and sustainable communities becomes a pressing one.

I was recently on my annual hiking vacation with friends in the Southwest. Talk about life and family, they are a married couple with two small children and we were out there camping and hiking. My life had to change to adapt to that. At one point we visited friends of theirs who have started what they call a "sustainable, fine restaurant" in the wilds of Utah, in a town called Boulder. If any of you know Utah, Boulder is really remote. They knew that they had been accepted by this community when they got a liquor license in very strong Mormon territory. What they've done is to establish their own farm, and they have set up a restaurant that is largely inspired by the Buddhist practice of the owners. They are trying to show people that you can eat well and you can eat graciously in an atmosphere that is rural, informal, and sustainable. It was really very inspiring. It is interesting that on their wall they had their story, which had appeared in Oprah's magazine. *New York Times* has been there. I marvel at people who would jet in to experience a sustainable dinner and then jet off. As I listened to the people and the commitment they had made to that town, which is about as foreign to their own background as you could find in the same country, and to what they were trying to do, I was edified. That's just one of thousands of examples of what people are trying to do in a myriad of ways. Who would have thought that somebody would try to prove this with a restaurant, but it was great. Because we were friends and despite the fact of our camping grubbies, we got to eat there. It was just one of those utterly memorable evenings to be in a place that felt so well tended in every dimension. So, there are good things happening out there. Let's just hope that we pull the frog out of the water before it is too late.

Global View of Monasticism Today

Abbot Primate Notker Wolf, OSB[1]

Introduction[2]

Notker Wolf, OSB, currently holds the position of Abbot Primate of the Benedictine Confederation. There is no such thing as a Benedictine Order, even though Benedictines identify themselves by using the initials OSB, *Ordo Santi Benedicti*, Order of Saint Benedict. The term "religious order" usually implies an international structure in which common observance is maintained through submission to a single authority figure, usually a superior general. But the Benedictine way of life does not really fit that institutional pattern. Monasteries are independent entities. Some would say "too independent." The Vatican thought so in the 1930s when it asked monasteries in the United States to collaborate in the establishment and staffing of a Catholic university in Beijing. Things did not go very well. At one point Pope Pius XI is reported to have cried out in exasperation to Abbot Alcuin Deutsch of Saint John's Abbey that the Benedictines were an order without order, *ordo sine ordine*.

1. Reverend Notker Wolf, OSB, was elected abbot of Saint Ottilien Abbey in Ammersee, Germany, in 1977. He was elected Abbot Primate of the Benedictine Confederation of abbots in 2000. He is a former professor of natural philosophy and scientific theory at the International Pontifical Benedictine College of Sant'Anselmo, Rome. He is also a gifted musician and has played with the rock group Feedback.

2. The Introduction of Abbot Primate Notker Wolf, OSB, by Reverend William Skudlarek, OSB, of Saint John's Abbey, provided helpful background about the history and role of Abbot Primate.

Monasteries, however, while safeguarding their autonomy, are grouped into congregations of men and federations of women. So the closest thing to an order for Benedictines would be a particular congregation or federation with its president and its own approach to living the Benedictine monastic way of life. In 1893 the various monastic congregations of men came together in a confederation approved by Pope Leo XIII. At the head of this worldwide Benedictine confederation is the Abbot Primate. Unlike the superior general of a religious order, the Abbot Primate has no jurisdiction over the presidents of the various Benedictine congregations and federations and thus with a few exceptions has no jurisdiction over individual monasteries.

Father Luke Dysinger of Valyermo identifies a major part of the Abbot Primate's responsibility as safeguarding the autonomy and the unique gifts possessed by the different congregations and federations and the monasteries that comprise them. Thus the role of the Abbot Primate is to promote harmony while protecting legitimate diversity. A few months after his election in 1967, Abbot Primate Rembert Weakland told me that he held a position of "great authority but of no jurisdiction." He went on to say that that is a wonderful model for how leadership could be exercised throughout the church. He leads by encouraging, supporting, fostering, promoting, cultivating, nurturing, cajoling, coaxing, persuading, sweet-talking, advising, counseling, instructing, informing, guiding, assisting, alerting, cautioning, and even warning Benedictine communities throughout the world rather than ordering or forcing them to do something.

For those of us who belong to the Benedictine family, Abbot Primate Notker Wolf is just such a leader. He exercises the authority with humor, enthusiasm, perseverance, and untold miles of travel. The story around Rome is that he is on a first-name basis with every single flight attendant on Lufthansa. There is really no one better qualified to give us a comprehensive and insightful global view of monasticism today.

Abbot Primate

Thank you, Father William, for your bright description of what an Abbot Primate is supposed to do. If you listen to the whole series of the epithets he gave us, you may think it's impossible, and as a matter of fact somehow it is impossible. I have two comforts: one is if you look at what Saint Benedict writes about what the abbot should do; it's also an impossible job. The second thing is, when Abbot Jerome Theisen was Abbot Primate, he set up a study group of about five or six people to write a new job description of the Abbot Primate to ease his job, but in the end, "the cat fell on its old feet," as we say. Perhaps if you were to watch *The Name of the Rose*, you could find all the projections of the people that are possible. Recently, many people have also come to Melk from the States after watching the *Da Vinci Code*, this secret code where the whole story is supposed to be written. They did not see that the whole thing is a fiction. So, I told the abbot, "You are a strange fellow; if you would have been in the Middle Ages and at least produced such a code, then you would have made money off it."

I will try to present the so-called Benedictine "disorder" as first-hand impressions, observations, and reflections. Some of what follows has been published in an article in the *Benedictines*,[3] the review of the Benedictine women here in the States. That discussion has continued with some excellent new contributions. Secondly, I should like to reflect especially on the Benedictine situation. "Global View of Monasticism Today" would practically involve all kinds of monasticisms—Buddhist, Hindu, etc.—but I don't feel competent to include all these monasticisms. It is important in such an Institute to reflect on our own Benedictine situation. First, I should like to give a statistical view of our situation. In a global view of monasticism today one could give figures and structures; this will be the first part of the presentation. But the second part is the life: the actual challenges and chances in different parts of the world and in general. Monasticism (or the monastic ideals, as we already heard) is ancient and at the same time always new. Its deep desire is the search for God in our hearts. And the ideals will be expressed in different times and different ways.

---

3. Notker Wolf, OSB, Abbot Primate, "Challenges Facing Benedictine Monasteries in the 21st Century," trans. Henry O'Shea, *Benedictines* 58, no.1 (Spring/Summer 2005): 6–19.

But if one looks back to history, the search for God has found quite a number of expressions. One of the major practical and realistic expressions has been the Rule of Saint Benedict (RB). But strange enough, there are so many ways to live out the Rule of Benedict; so the art and leadership of an Abbot Primate should be to integrate these many ways of living out the Rule of Benedict. There have always been tendencies in our Benedictine history to say, "We are the world, we are the real Benedictines, and the other ones are not real Benedictines." When I was younger, I would be angry at these things. Nowadays, I just keep smiling and say, "If you need that for your identity to survive, then you may have it." Very often, the real life or the real search for God is found in perhaps a precarious small community that is just trying to live out the Gospel. That's all.

Statistics Concerning Benedictine Communities around the World

Now about statistics. Soon the long-awaited *Catalogus 2005* and also the *Catalogus* of Benedictine Women will be published, which is being prepared by the Benedictine women themselves, the Kommunität Venio in Munich, a Secular Institute. The reason why it takes so much time to publish this document is that every line must be verified, and given the fact that there are about 7,500 members in our Benedictine confederation, the verification and corrections take a long time. And there are more than double the number of Benedictine women: 17,100. Whereas the Benedictine men have decreased by about 1,000 within the last five years (although exact figures are not sure), Benedictine women have increased by about 500.

The Benedictine men are organized in twenty congregations as a result of the will of Pope Leo XIII. He said that too much autonomy may cause harm to a monastery. A monastery can be isolated and can lose its discipline, its personnel, and its money. So, he encouraged monks to stick together in congregations, to have more of the same orientation, not always of the same region in this world, and to help each other to have a general check, to have an Abbot President (and his council) who takes care of the congregation. Perhaps we should do even more. Just this morning I was confronted with the situation of a German monastery that is in great difficulty, a beautiful monastery. There are only a few young monks left who it seems don't see their responsibility for the future of this monastery. They are not mature enough, and the abbot who is now the administrator may not also see how precarious their situation is. We have no people to send there. But anyhow, this was one of the problems involved in the reason why Leo XIII wanted to unite the Benedictines as an order as he had done with the Franciscans. But the abbots resisted and only accepted an Abbot Primate without any power. When people ask me to explain my authority, I say that the power of the Abbot Primate is the powerlessness. But perhaps that's also very evangelical if you think of 1 Corinthians 1.

Now the Benedictine women are more than double the size of the men. Why is that? As mentioned earlier, usually women have double the number that men do in religious life. I reflect that women are far closer to life, far more sensitive to life and also to the origin of life. Therefore, they have a stronger, that is, more open access to God as the creator of life. And therefore they are much more open toward God than men. Men are more on the external side and unfortunately they love fighting until the eruption of war. Ja!

What about the women's organization? Fortunately we succeeded in 2001 in Nairobi to set up a *Communio Internationalis Benedictinarum* [CIB] comprised of nineteen regions of Benedictine women who are now gathered under this spiritual umbrella. They are not a real organization, but a communion. For Benedictine women the term "union" sounded too juridical, so they chose a term that expressed more their spiritual unity. Their coordinator is Mother Mairé Hickey, an Irish abbess in Germany, of a German abbey.

Now the situation of Benedictine women is far more divergent than among men. Among men everywhere the structure of the monasteries is practically the same. With Benedictine women, one big distinction is between nuns and sisters. The nuns live in cloister. Some of them have joined the monastery sixty, seventy years ago and have never left their monastery, whereas the Benedictine sisters go out, doing lots of excellent work. These are different charisms. There has been some link with the sisters at Eichstätt, who were allowed to go out and teach although they are cloistered nuns. But their teaching tradition is older than the papal enclosure, also an interesting phenomenon. Usually the sisters are organized in autonomous federations or papal congregations like the Tutzing Missionary Benedictine Sisters. The nuns are usually under the bishops and some are not looking to the future. They have now set up federations in some places, like in Italy and Spain, but they are by no means nearly as strong as the Benedictine federations here in the United States. They don't have their proper authority, just a loose organization. It will be illusionary for the near future to have a counterpart on the female side to an Abbot Primate, that is, to have, for example, an Abbess Primatissa, because the situation is so variegated and changeable. There are now nuns' monasteries completely incorporated into male monastic congregations such as in the Beuronese, Brazilian, and the English congregations. There the abbesses have the same rights as abbots except for becoming an Abbot President.[4] But they have extensive rights in the council of the congregation and also for canonical visitations. As yet we have not reflected on what that means to the situation of the Benedictine Confederation, which up until now had just been a male construct. At least there is some movement, some development going on, and law always comes afterward. Hopefully, law does not block reality. Now let us see something about the structures.

Structures for Benedictine Men and Women

There are many associations or assemblies on a regional, national, continental, or even international basis. For example, the abbots' workshop in the United States meets every year, the prioresses also meet every year, and every third or fourth year the two groups meet together. In Latin America, in November 2006, there will be the meeting of the EMLA (Encuentro Monastico Latino Americano), all the representatives of the Benedictine, Cistercian, and Trappist monasteries, both the sisters and brothers. Each has its own house

---

4. Cf. Wolf, "Challenges," 13.

tradition, but in reality they are very close to each other, like a really big family. But this is perhaps also a reflection of an enculturation of our monastic charism into the Latin American situation. There are also the Mexican Benedictine Association, the Brazilian, and the ABECA (Benedictine Association of the Caribbean and Andes).

Another that meets every year is in India, the Indian-Sri Lankan Benedictine Federation. This year that federation set up a mobile monastic institute. Abbot John from Kappadu is a tough, visionary man, but also very realistic, who has said what they need basically is a solid formation. That has always been true in the past for any kind of reform: a beginning starts with a solid formation. He said, "But in India we want to do it ourselves according to our Indian culture and we don't like to go around always begging, but we really want to see what *we* can do." He knew that they don't have the money to set up a whole school, as, for example, here in Saint John's. But what they can do every year is offer a six-week course in a different place. So, each year one of the houses pays for the living expenses of the course there. Their own fellows, who have studied in Rome and elsewhere, teach, and sometimes they find some other Indian scholar or one or two from the Benedictine confederation to teach. Doing it for themselves and soliciting their own forces challenges them. I am very happy about such an example, for it is based on *lectio divina*, which is the title of their institute. That means that they are studying what *lectio divina* is through biblical studies, patristics, and modern spiritual literature. The course will extend over three years. They decided in February 2006 and have already in May started the first session with thirty-seven participants. Also amazing is that in India the whole presence of the Benedictines is growing continuously, especially with the Indian monasteries establishing new foundations.

Then there is in the Far East the Benedictine East Asian Commission or organization, which includes the Pacific and meets every second year. In South Africa there is the BECOSA, the Benedictine Communities of Southern Africa.

In Europe there are several unions, the most important one being the conference of Salzburg, the union of all abbots of German language. They meet every year after Easter. The Italian abbots have been encouraged to do the same because of a number of problems that monasteries will face there in the future. Among the French there is the Union monastique. The Spanish and Portuguese have their encounter every three years. Now in Poland, Benedictines are also meeting every year. There are around one thousand Benedictines in Poland, about whom not so much is known. There are monasteries in the former Soviet Union countries. There are also two women's monasteries in Lithuania, and Solesme has also founded a men's monastery in Lithuania. For the rest, there are fewer foundations in Eastern Germany, where the Jesuits and Silesians have been far stronger. Finally, there is some revival in the Slav congregations.

The Czech monasteries present a very onerous situation because it is difficult to set up an old kind of monastery in a whole society that has changed. The first real candidates are arriving at the three monasteries in the Czech Republic. The Tihany Monastery has set up the first real foundation in Slovakia, and the nuns from Offida in Italy are also starting a nuns' monastery in Slovakia. In Munich, three Czech sisters are slowly moving to start a Benedictine monastery in Prague. One Italian monastery has started a foundation in Romania, where there is a second Romanian monastery. The Tutzing Missionary Benedictine Sisters have remained in Bulgaria since the First World War, throughout that whole difficult period, with the hope of getting new vocations there.

There are also institutions within our confederations, the main one being AIM [Alliance for International Monasticism]; it is not only Benedictine but also includes the collaboration of Cistercians and Trappists. The same holds true for the Monastic Interreligious Dialogue; both institutions began in the early 1960s. Then there is the Benedictine Commission on China, which recently set up an international commission on Benedictine education. All these facts give an idea of the figures and structure of the Benedictines.

Activities of Benedictines

Many monasteries have now given up farming, gardening, and workshops that were so Benedictine throughout the ages. However, in the poor countries they should nevertheless continue to do these works. First of all, they need these activities for their own maintenance.

The most important activity is our schools, in which approximately 150,000 young people around the world are being taught. In a secularizing globalization it will be even more important to be aware of our Benedictine profile in order to share some values with our world, especially as a kind of mission. Moreover, there are a few trade or agricultural schools.

Among other endeavors are guesthouses for preaching retreats and giving conferences. There are still many parishes in some congregations, although the number is decreasing because the number of vocations is declining, at least among Benedictine men. But what is less well known is the care of some very important places of pilgrimage and important shrines. First of all, there is the Dormition Abbey in Jerusalem, on the place where Our Lady is said to have died, located next to the Cenacle, the place of the Last Supper. Dormition is a major place of Christian memory. But also Saint Paul's Outside the Walls has the tomb of Saint Paul. The community there has been consolidated with collaboration from several monasteries; more collaboration will be needed in the future in terms of vocations for this international community, where monks have been living for thirteen hundred years. There is also the Apostles' tomb, Saint Matthias, in Korea.

One should not forget Santiago de Compostela in Spain. The whole movement was initiated by Cluny when it built the old cathedral there, which is now inside the Baroque Cathedral. In addition, Cluny built several churches along the pilgrimage way to Santiago de Compostela. It is amazing considering the fact that Cluny is usually portrayed by the Solesme Congregation as an outstanding model of contemplative life—not leaving the monastery. But nuns and monks nonetheless love to move around. There are also other shrines like Montserrat, Maria Einsiedeln, Montevergine, and, of course, the outstanding shrine at Monte Cassino. This latter shrine has become a symbol both of the absurdity of war and of Benedictine peace.

So, Benedictines are not shrinking that much nor are they becoming meaningless in this world, although meaningless could be a positive way of humility. Then there are the printing presses and all the services to the mass media, as for example in the abbey in South Korea. With regard to hospitals, the sisters of Tutzing are outstanding, especially with their hospital in China. There is another interesting hospital in Ewu-Ishan in Nigeria, founded by the monks there, where the second biggest herbal clinic of Africa is located and it is still increasing. They serve at least a hundred pharmacies or more in their country. These increasing businesses in our Benedictine world leave me breathless. It may create some problems later on because we used to say, "small is beautiful." But it is not always true, because living in a small community you step on each other's feet very easily. In a larger community there is much more space.

Challenges in the Benedictine World

Among the global challenges, we will first address those in different parts of the Benedictine world and then those in general. There are lots of problems if one looks around, but this is a normal sign of life. It is part of the process of enculturation of our Benedictine way of life into different cultures, but also into the modern, secularized culture. Second, I see much movement and much crisis, but these are signs of life. One can sometimes have a strange, deep desire for harmony in a community where we are all sitting together and singing in one voice. But one can also have a desire for harmony in a historical sense, in which one thinks that the problems are settled forever and there are no more problems, only a continuing on. This is what traditionalists are always hoping when they look back, as if there should not be any new development. So, a few of the problems will be highlighted here.

In Latin America, one of the major problems is perseverance of vocations, which is not the problem only of monastic vocations. Around 1980 it was reported that about 35 percent of religious priest vocations were leaving their jobs, probably caused by the whole cultural situation there, where people are coming from broken families. Young people are not experiencing a real sense of stability. Rather, they are experiencing how their fathers left their families and were looking for other wives. Fidelity does not seem to be a significant value. Then a second problem is the fact that monasteries are increasing in members again but not too quickly. Most have been founded by different European or American monasteries, but now they are looking for their real Latin American identity, which is not easy to identify. They will need time to adapt and adjust to each other. Therefore, that is one of the reasons one does not find big differences between Benedictines, Cistercians, and Trappists, who feel like one great monastic family. Some but not many are running schools. They love the small communities and the smaller monasteries more. The Benedictine women are very strong there, especially the cloistered nuns, but also the active sisters.

Africa is a special situation. There are quite a number of men's communities, many of which have serious problems. As in Latin America, there is a question of perseverance, of stability. But Africans are asking: "Do you belong to a new family? Is this one stronger, or is your old one?" The questions have not yet been resolved in the hearts of many. Becoming Benedictine should be about creating a new family. But the Zimbabwean Jesuits told me once, "You cannot believe how strong the bonds to our families are in our bones. We have to respect and to cope with such a situation." Another problem is celibacy, which is different for women and men. There are different attitudes toward sexuality in different tribes. There are monogamous tribes; there are tribes where you can easily have a second wife. It's not so important that a man has some relationship to a woman in a kind of responsible way. Something still has to grow. In Ndanda the sisters told me that especially the natural way of birth control is creating a new attitude between man and woman: the man finally has to respect the woman and not just use the woman, even if she is his own wife. So, one sees that a new meaning of sexuality, what it really means to integrate this strong and valuable power into one's own personality, is a challenge. Key challenges in African monasteries include money, attitudes toward women, and perseverance. Another major challenge has to do with monasteries that have been created with an unclear identity. The Europeans arrived there and set up monasteries and thought the Africans would just follow the same line. But in the meantime, the social situation has changed completely. So, they have to find their new identity. The same was true in the monastery in Waegwan, Korea, whose members will have to find out their new way. Even the French monasteries in West Africa are undergoing similar problems, because the French also thought the ideal way of Benedictine life was the French way. The same is true of the Germans and Swiss in East Africa. There is still a long way to go. But one should not despair, for in Europe it took centuries. It took a long time here in the United States until you found your own way. The situation is different because you are now a mixed population here, coming from different countries, whereas in Africa, monasticism was implanted into a population that did not know monasticism.

Now with respect to India, Benedictines are growing. There is an attitude one encounters, "In India the Benedictines have nothing to say. We should just set up ashrams." While that might be good, the ashram, nevertheless, is a reflection of the Hindu system based on castes. The focus in on the top: one guru and all the people gathered around him. This is not Benedictine. The abbot is not the guru; he is the Vicar of Christ in a community, to lead it. What is so important in the Benedictine way of life, which is a very Christian understanding, is the communal, the ecclesial aspect of our life. Benedictines are not just religious, with the contact between the monastic and God, but it is so important to live in community. This message has to be brought to India without disrespecting the high values of Indian culture. Another positive value is that of manual labor, which in India is for the lower castes; the higher castes are also working but they do not like to get their hands dirty.

Then looking to the continental Far East, where there is the Confucian tradition, even there the real sense of a fraternal community is sounding most important. Benedictines can show that our obedience, which is not just linked with hierarchy, is one of faith. In the Philippines, the problem is again one of perseverance in this society caused in part because there are strong Benedictine women in the Philippines, yet Benedictine men are far weaker. Because of the matriarchy in the families, the woman has the say and the male being cannot develop very well.

Now finally in the Western societies, monastic members, and so monasteries, are shrinking. It is in part a milieu that is nonreligious, even antireligious, at least in Europe, and secularized. People say life without God is the real life and therefore the pope is strongly attacking this dictatorship of relativism. The highest value, people say, is individual freedom. The human becomes the real creator of his or her own future, not only of the world in techniques but also morals. This milieu creates lots of problems because there is not an environment where religious vocations can easily grow. Then there is the whole demographic situation. For example, in Germany there is a growth of the population of -0.5 among Catholics; in Italy it is the same; and Poland has the highest number of abortions. So, where will religious vocations come from? The New Age and many religious tendencies represent a patchwork religiosity where everybody is looking for his or her own God. Each one is determining how God is allowed to look and creating his or her own religion. Real service to a creator of this world and to our Savior is so far away from their thinking. So, these are influences in the milieu.

A second area of concern is our monasteries, which, instead of being full of life, have become institutions in many cases where every individual is just a functioning member. Where is the chance then for new movements and new communities? Some say that this cannot be religious life if you think of Jesus and his structures. In Germany, if one would like to live out serious religious life, one would first look for an institution and for some laws rather than to search out a kind of freedom one can experience with Jesus. Of course, some monasteries have realized the situation and have come to some reform. Then the bigger problem is the number of precarious communities, or rather, if leadership does not like to face reality, they are still closing their eyes. When nuns in Italy told me, "Yes, we are waiting for new vocations; God can create new vocations just out of stones," I said, "Mother, I admire your faith, but why didn't God do so up till now already?"[5] One needs to face the situation where there are only two ways out. First, one needs to see that if there is no way

5. Ibid., 9.

out of a renewal, then one may look for a human end with dignity. Some still reduce everything and do not inquire if what they are doing is edifying in their lives or for the people who meet them. Fortunately, a number of laypeople, who are much more down to earth than these holy nuns, help them very often. But also one could ask, "OK, this kind of service has passed. What's necessary now?" Schools and hospitals for the most part have been taken over by the state or by other private institutions. The Benedictine message can be put forward there, yes, with some other challenges, but also as real signs of hope.

General Challenges

Now among the general challenges is life in a democratic society, where there is no longer a sense for obedience, and people are more focused on individual freedom. Individualism is found in many monasteries where many monks (more so than Benedictine women) are living out their own way of life, no longer in a communitarian spirit. Another problem inside communities is the mediocrity of the lifestyle, something the pope has been criticizing. One only has to think about the whole question of the internet and the downloading of porn.

Benedictines need very mature characters in communities with a formation toward maturity, not just an external obedience of following the same line. It is so important to provide an emotional maturity where members can really find out their way in community. One of the best helps is to live in community, because then there will be some kind of social control, which we frail human beings need. There is also need for a kind of manual of ascetic life or ascetic rules. This idea is not to fall back into negativism but in order to save our freedom: to get free and to remain free. To abstain from certain foods and so on should show that one is still free. Something may be beautiful, but it is not necessary to us.

Then another challenge is a low level of formation, a problem particular to many women's communities. They have been the servants of God: when they were able to clean shoes and make beds, it was just sufficient. In some communities there was the problem of trained sisters and untrained sisters. Now in our democracy, it should be possible to overcome all these problems, but there are human tendencies that block efforts.

For example, the clericalism among monks' monasteries is horrible, especially in Africa and India, where one very often sees the monk as just another kind of priest. But one can look into communities all around the world where the number of lay monks is comparatively low to the general number. Another new problem is our multicultural and multireligious society. At least this challenge has brought us to helpful dialogue, for dialogue fosters one's own identity, one's own self-understanding, but also tolerance, esteem, and appreciation of other religions to live together in peace.

Another challenge is the effect of immigration. Our world is fast becoming a world of migration. Last week in Erie I saw what the sisters are doing, for example, to integrate those immigrants, legal or illegal. In my own monastery we had a group of illegal immigrants for six years, eight Muslims, a Kurd family that was fighting with our minister of the interior. In the end they went to Poland where they are surviving and we keep in close contact with them.

Another problem of our modern time is the world economy, in which one feels helpless. The best thing is to find either big business or some niches where one can foster ecological, biological agriculture. Many sisters' and nuns' monasteries are living from processed products, like marmalades, honey, candles. But will these activities provide a real future?

Chances and Hopes

So, many challenges and problems have been mentioned, but they are signs of life. One can see the whole under the umbrella of the church. The church itself has so many problems all over the world. Even if Catholics are happy now to have had John Paul II, who made a great impression worldwide, and Benedict XVI is well respected, Vatican II has given the definition that the church is on pilgrimage. It is a wandering church, not just a simple structure, not a saint society; rather, it is on the move. The people of the desert, that is, Israel in the desert, are my vision for individual monasteries, but also for the confederation and for the CIB, the women's communion. Now Benedictines are going through the desert somehow and looking for answers to these challenges. Today we may find an answer that is already wrong tomorrow.

For traditionalists, respect is due to them, for they want a really serious life without mediocrity, which is a very good intention that should challenge us all. But, on the other hand, the answer cannot be just that of 1940; their answers are historical answers of a certain period. Certainly there are basic monastic elements that hold true throughout the whole of history, like the basic principles that Saint Benedict gives in the beginning of his Rule: the first about the four types of monks, next authority, then integrating the whole group of monastics into the decisions and into the life of a community. This sense of the whole community had been forgotten in the past when too much decision making was concentrated in the authority, with a distraction between those in authority and those who are under the authority. The authority thought *for* the community instead of *with* the community. Moreover, silence, humility, reading, liturgical prayer, and working are all principles. But principles are not all yet complete forms, for they materialize in each period in a different way. Benedictines have to be rather self-critical and ask, "Are we still fulfilling the original ideal, the original vision of monasticism?"

Despite shrinking numbers, one very good sign for the future is the reform of liturgy. Wherever I go, the celebrations of liturgy are very decent and edifying. A quiet, solemn, simple liturgy is so important. Then there is a new appreciation of *lectio divina*: if *lectio divina* is done every day, it will transform our life progression.

Another progress is that Benedictines have become more aware of the communal aspect of our life. Yet we could learn from the new communities and new movements: to give each other time to live together. For example, instead of each individual member being head of departments in a hospital, the Franciscan sisters in Germany chose to take over the pastoral responsibility in the hospital. This change means that they have time now for communal life, prayer, meditation, and sharing.

Another development is hospitality in our guest and retreat houses where much dialogue is going on both on the ecumenical level and on the interreligious level. In monasteries people usually come and feel welcome because no ideology is put on them. They are allowed to live there and to reflect. This is so important for younger people. In my monastery in Germany, among others, there is a new movement. Twenty years ago, about fifteen to twenty young people came to say, "We also want to sing Vespers. Not the way you are doing it; for us the psalms are too difficult to understand, but let us sing together and pray together, listen to the word of God and some good sermons." So, they came for twenty years, every First Friday of the month. I always said, "Come over to join our community and we would adapt ourselves to you." But they said, "No, it's so beautiful in our Ottilien chapel, it's a baroque chapel." They feel together because it is a little bit cozy there and they loved it. But in the year 2000 the father in charge of this group came during supper to see me and said, "Father, tonight we cannot sing Compline in our church; we have occupied the church, the number has grown." And in the meantime, every First Friday, more than one thousand young people are coming from all over Bavaria, to meet, to pray for two hours, and to exchange their ideas afterwards when they are sitting together in groups. All this happened without any publicity in Münsterschwarzach and other monasteries, too. People are longing for a place where they find contact with God in the place of human community. In the meantime a group of young couples from the first group, who started the Vespers and have grown older, meet once a month on Sunday afternoon while our young confreres take care of their kids. There are movements out there if we are open enough, if we are listening to the Holy Spirit. The same holds true for our schools where the Benedictine profile is being developed, not just teaching but forming characters.

Another movement that gives hope are the oblates. Recently the Oblates Congress had a far bigger echo than one would ever have thought. Preparations for the next one are taking place after a short rest and reflection.

Some Words about Sant'Anselmo

And last but not least, a word about Sant'Anselmo. Sant'Anselmo is a kind of meeting point where all these problems and all these hopes are coming together. It is the meeting place for the Abbots' Congress, the Women's Symposium, representatives of the oblates, and our university. At the university we have basic formation: thirty-five nations are living there together day by day, washing dishes together, serving each other at table (it is beautiful), praying together; one hundred twenty people, professors, and students.

The university has four hundred fifty students coming from eighty nations. Half of them are studying in the liturgical institute. It is also a place for training future leaders. Quite a number of abbots or other leaders have passed through this place. In this year already seven alumni of the liturgical institute have been appointed bishops. This has not been our aim—to train bishops; however, it is not too bad if a bishop understands something of liturgy. On the whole, Sant'Anselmo is an amazing place.

Sant'Anselmo has a very frail existence, a very humble place, for it is not strong. Even the roof is not strong; part of it collapsed recently. Fortunately nobody was hurt. But we are continuing to serve our whole Benedictine "disorder." In the beginning, mention was made about the many jobs, or the great authority the Abbot Primate has. This has been my policy, that it is not just the Abbot Primate's responsibility for the Benedictine Confederation; it is the responsibility of all the abbots. There is need for much more collaboration, not just among the Benedictine men, but this should also grow among Benedictine women. We need time for that, because if one has lived in a certain lifestyle for a long time, one cannot change it just from today to tomorrow. But Benedictines have to learn to reflect, to talk to each other, and I think, in this regard, Sant'Anselmo is a point of discussion, is a point of meeting, of studies and reflection, and provides a real service to the whole confederation. My hope is that we are going through this desert of our world with great optimism because this desert has been created by God. Sometimes, when I am meeting people, and they are very crazy, I think, "But they are also being created by God. God, what did you think when you created them? Have you fallen asleep?" And perhaps God had been falling asleep when God created me. Thank you very much.

Dialogue with Abbot Primate Notker Wolf, OSB

A request for more information about Sant'Anselmo

Sant'Anselmo was created by Pope Leo XIII, who loved the Benedictines, especially in their renewal period. He said first of all that the Benedictines should get more organized; second, they should have a common study and monastic center in Rome. So, he bought a beautiful plot on the Aventine Hill, which at the time was outside Rome; now it is sitting in an expensive residential area of Rome. Although there were already other universities in Rome—the Gregorianum, Franciscan University, the Lateran, and Urbaniana—he had an idea to unify the daily way of the Benedictine lifestyle during the strong time of the Beuronese Congregation. Many customs of the Beuronese Congregation were taken over by a number of monasteries, which even influenced some monasteries in the United States. But they did not reflect the local cultures. While one can live out the common Benedictine principles, one cannot live out the same lifestyle. Even in the same country, Sankt Ottilien in Bavaria is so different from Jakobsberg in Northern Germany and from Münsterschwarzach. Pope Leo had the idea in this revival of Benedictine life—Dom Prosper Guéranger in France and Boniface Wimmer in America, Maurus and Placid Wolter in Beuron, Andreas Amrhein in Sankt Ottilien, and Jean-Baptiste Muard in La Pierre-qui-Vire—to coordinate these different movements. Nowadays it is necessary to live in a global village and to foster each other. In the monastic life, autonomy is very important; however, too much autonomy, too much independence, can mean isolation and death. This balance in a congregation of living together and helping each other, but also respecting the individual character of each monastery, is a special, human art. This model could offer a right way of international politics for the future: the goal of respecting individual identity, but also solidarity, living in community, like in a family.

So, Sant'Anselmo has developed from its origin of fifty to sixty students to the current four hundred fifty with no more space in the house. The building, a hundred twenty years old, while beautiful, is falling apart. Many renovations are going on; the workers have to abide by the trade unions and the new laws in Europe. I would like to see more Benedictine women studying there for the future, but the problem is one of financing, for a university costs a lot. When I was teaching at Sant'Anselmo, because my salary was one hundred euros per month plus room and board, I survived on support from my abbey and by serving as a tour guide for some groups. Monasteries pay a tax per capita each year equal to forty-two U.S. dollars, which yields about three hundred thousand euros per year; this amount will decrease because there will be one thousand fewer people. Although we have a solidarity fund, I set up the PIL (Pontifical Institute of Liturgy) Foundation for Sant'Anselmo and the Saint Benedict Foundation for Education. For developing our faculty, we are discussing, with the International Rotary Club, to set up a new Department of Religion and Peace.

Sant'Anselmo has three faculties: (1) philosophy, with specialization in philosophy and mystics; (2) theology, with specialization in sacramental theology, history of theology (not the history of the church), and a monastic institute; and (3) an institute of liturgy founded by Pope John XXIII in 1961. Specialized courses for the vicariate of Rome train over two hundred people for liturgical services in parishes who come once a week for three years and receive a special document. Twenty architects come for a course on liturgy and architecture.

About one hundred twenty monks in the house are under the prior, Father Michael Naughton, from Saint John's Abbey. He had to study Italian. He radiates a calm atmosphere there. The leadership represents a completely international group: an Italian vice-prior; an American rector, Father Mark Sheridan; a Dutch Trappist as dean of theology; an Italian dean of philosophy; and myself—a Bavarian.

No new buildings are allowed because we are in an archeological zone, although we are permitted to dig out the cloister, to extend the library, and to have a big hall for three hundred people. Hopefully, the major part of the money will come from the ministry of culture, but first the whole roof has to be repaired because it is falling apart, at a cost of three million euros.

What about small communities and their renewal of life?

First, the small communities are not always very alive. Small is not always beautiful because your feet are so close. On the other hand, a family life can develop there, where each member feels a need to make a contribution to the community. That is why Saint Benedict wanted deaneries in a larger community; we should set up deaneries so a member doesn't disappear in an anonymous big community. Some people like to disappear to avoid the challenge. In a smaller community one is challenged very much. In one such community in Germany, no one is missing at the Morning Office, because they need each other to be there. It is more concrete, like in a family, where the man does not want to get out of bed in the morning, but his wife kicks him out of bed to go to work. Only in a monastery can one be lazy. Also, members can sit together and talk at breakfast or after breakfast: "What are you doing today?" It is important in a small community to give room to each other; to keep the distance. Monks are not married. On the other hand, if it works well, it needs a lot of tolerance, just as for married couples. For me it was really amazing when I saw my classmates from elementary school and high school— how much these demanding men changed when they got married. They had to withdraw, hand in their money, accept, and become much more humble. They became much more humble than monks have become.

Larger communities have great advantages, for example, for solemn celebrations. They can do lots of things that small communities cannot do. After Vatican II we said, "only small is beautiful," but later on we saw that people are also flocking to larger communities because of so many possibilities.

As an example of a renewed community, I think of the monastery of Offida, which has been inspired by the charismatic Pentecostal movement and has given a new life to the whole community for living out the Gospel. The new ones are challenging the older ones. They have refounded the new community of Prague, which had gone down to two to three nuns; now they are fourteen. There is joy in that cloistered monastery. What did the abbess do? "We have such a nice veranda in the summer, we go there to do embroidery; we have a chance to talk to each other, to have recreation without artificial recreation." Despite recreation being one of the most problematic institutions in our monasteries, there is a real life there with singing of modern songs.

Another women's monastery in North Italy—Isola San Giulio— has a very spiritual abbess; so many young women are flocking there. She does not train them in an infantile way. They find a spiritual life and joy of community in their work. They started a new community two years ago in Wilda Austa. She told me they would never start from an old monastery, whereas Offida helps out older monasteries, like in the Diocese of Tierney, where one of the founders came from Sant'Egidio.

Sometimes for the revival of a community it is better to die out, especially if there is no more challenge or if there is a stiffness in the psychological structure. I see hope in communities where there is a center of a solemn, good liturgy, not in the *quantum* but the quality, that is, taking time to celebrate—not preserve the liturgy and the community—and being with people. The model of pastoral service is Jesus sitting together with his people. That is the model of an abbot, sitting together with his apostles or disciples, knowing that even he is not Jesus, but Jesus is sitting in the middle of them. Gaining back our spiritual view in our monasteries will change them over time. Leaving it open to the Holy Spirit, not being efficient, will show the joy of living together and the joy of living out the Gospel.

What is your vision for formation of oblates and their integration into monasteries in our world?

It is a great pity that there are still communities with oblates where the monastics have no relation with them. That's a great pity. Monastics still remain in this world. It is like Moses going through the desert with his people: the core group is the monastic group with the people around them. The core group becomes attractive to other people, as stable points from whom people find some spiritual food. This has been the main idea behind the founding of monasteries throughout the ages. People who are looking for an orientation say, "Please give us also some of the food, some bread that you are eating." How rich is this mission of the monasteries! We are just one, one Body of Christ. Nobody should tell the other, "I do not need you." We have to help each other. A monastic community, by living together, has something special to give and should do so. On the other hand, the oblates are already sharing the prayer life of the monastic community, which was the ideal of Vatican II. In Saint Ottilien, the oblates feel united to a real community. In the evening or in the morning they take the breviary and pray at home and feel united with the community. The monastic community should be most grateful for people who are thinking and praying for them. To live with God in a Benedictine way is a special spirituality, a natural living with God, our Creator and our Savior, which gives a special dimension to our life. If oblates also can hand it on to other oblates with the support of the monastery, this is real Christian life.

The Sign of Jonah
and a New Monasticism

Jonathan Wilson-Hartgrove[1]

I am a representative of the Rutba House, a new monastic community in Durham, North Carolina. The celebration of one hundred fifty years at Saint John's is a reminder to me of just how new we are. We've only been around for three years. The Rutba House takes its name from a little town in the western desert of Iraq, where my wife Leah and I were at the beginning of the U.S.-led invasion of Iraq with a group called the Christian Peacemaker Teams. When American friends of ours were seriously injured in a car accident, some Iraqis stopped by the roadside and picked them up. They carried our bleeding friends to this town called Rutba. When they got there the doctor said to them, "Three days ago your country bombed our hospital, but we will take care of you." He sewed up their heads and saved their lives. When I asked the doctor what we owed him for his services, he said, "Nothing. Please just tell the world what has happened in Rutba."

---

1. Jonathan Wilson-Hartgrove, a preacher, writer, and Christian peacemaker, is a founding member of the Rutba House community in Durham, North Carolina. He is a graduate of Eastern University and Duke Divinity School. The book *New Monasticism*, which he edited, was the result of several people coming together at Durham in June 2004 to talk about the twelve marks of new monasticism, as the Spirit leads Christian communities into creative expressions of ecumenical Christian living.

The more we told that story after returning from Iraq, the more we realized that it was a Good Samaritan story. The Iraqis, who were supposed to be our enemies, had stopped by the roadside, pulled our friends out of the ditch, and saved their lives. God gave us a sign of his love and sent a Good Iraqi to teach us how to love our neighbors as ourselves. We knew that we had to find a way to live into that love back here in America.

So, we started a little community of hospitality and called it Rutba House. A couple of folks came to join us, and we were energized by the thought that our faith could become a way of life. But we didn't know what we were doing. We did sense that we were part of something larger than ourselves. So, we wrote to every intentional Christian community, live-in church, Protestant order, and conventional monastery we knew of and asked them to join us in Durham for a time of discernment about what the Holy Spirit is up to in America. About seventy-five folks came from a dozen or so communities.

After four days of talking, listening, praying, and eating together, the group discerned twelve practices that mark new communities like ours in the United States today. Stories of others from other places resonated with our story at Rutba House. Scholars among us who knew church history recognized in our stories streams that run deep in the church's story. We committed ourselves to dig deep in the Scriptures and tradition for wisdom that would help us live into the long history of Israel and the church. The more we dug, the more we sensed ourselves caught up in a movement that we dubbed a "new monasticism."[2]

In Matthew's gospel, Jesus rebukes the scribes and Pharisees when they ask him for a sign. He shoots back an accusation: they do not know how to read the signs of the times. He is frustrated because the Pharisees can't see what God is doing. For all their study of Scripture, they do not know God when they meet him face-to-face. How could a sign help them when they fail to recognize God in human flesh? The only sign they will be given, Jesus says, is the sign of Jonah.

---

2. See *School(s) for Conversion: 12 Marks of a New Monasticism*, ed. Rutba House, New Monastic Library: Resources for Radical Discipleship (Eugene, OR: Cascade Books/Wipf and Stock Publishers, 2005).

The sign of Jonah is an allusion to Jesus' resurrection after three days in the grave, just as Jonah was three days in the belly of the fish before God had him spit out on the shore. "The life of every monk, of every priest, of every Christian," Thomas Merton wrote, "is signed with the sign of Jonah. . . ." We are a resurrection people, marked by the gift of new creation. But Merton also reminds us of the tension in Jonah's story: "Like Jonas himself," Merton said, "I find myself traveling toward my destination in the belly of a paradox."[3]

The new monasticism can be described today as a witness to the Holy Spirit's work in the belly of the paradox called America. It is a way of life that our communities have received as good news right here in the midst of the world's last remaining superpower. This statement certainly does not mean to say that the Holy Spirit is not at work outside America—just that, for better or worse, this is where we have sojourned. If the new monasticism is a movement, it is more like a river that we have fallen into than a march that we organized. We stumbled into this way of life by the grace of God and continued efforts to practice the gift of resurrection in the belly of the beast.

In short, to use Matthew's language, we got to where we are by trying to read the signs of the times. Three of those signs will be mentioned today: Iraq, Katrina, and immigration, which are indicative signs of the twenty-first century. First, there is Iraq. The United States declared war on terror in 2001 and said that our national security demanded aerial bombardment, invasion, and occupation of Iraq in 2003. Leaders of almost every major denomination of the church said that such a war would be unjust. Nevertheless, hundreds of thousands of Christians were deployed to the Middle East and have fought a war whose futility is increasingly manifest to a majority of Americans. Now it is important that we read the sign carefully. I do not want to be another liberal who says America was imprudent and all we need is a new president in 2008. My point is not to argue politics (at least, not in any conventional sense). My point is to say that Iraq is a sign of the times for Christians. That the American church was powerless

3. Thomas Merton, *The Sign of Jonas* (New York: Image Books, 1956), 7.

to do what its just-war tradition and all its bishops said it should do in Iraq shows us just how hard it is to be Christian in America.

Katrina is another sign. America will not soon forget those pictures of desperate black faces in the Superdome, looking as if they had caught a glimpse of hell. Of course, by now the dead have been buried, the homeless relocated, the emergency relieved. And our churches have demonstrated a great deal of compassion in ministries of hospitality, relief, and reconstruction. We feel better about Katrina. But we cannot let our ministry keep us from reading this sign of the times. Katrina exposes the persistence of white supremacy and economic disparity in the Body of Christ. I heard a story about a white minister in North Carolina who, when he saw the initial news coverage of Katrina, commented to his wife that he didn't know New Orleans was such a black city. Of course, it wasn't. Poor African Americans were left behind by fellow citizens of New Orleans who only thought to look out for themselves. But again, horrible as it is, human selfishness should not surprise us. We know that people are broken by sin. This is the real tragedy: not many white Christians stopped on their way out of New Orleans to offer a ride to their black sisters and brothers. The tragedy is that it didn't even occur to them— and that it most likely would not occur to us if Katrina happened in our towns. Katrina is a sign to us that, when the pressure is on, we Christians have not learned to love one another as Christ loved us.

Quickly, a third sign is the current immigration debate. Within the logic of nation-state politics and democratic capitalism, it makes sense that a country must defend its borders, control immigration, and protect its economic interests. Debates between liberals and conservatives in American politics have been about how best to do this. But as people adopted into the family of God, we share our most fundamental citizenship with brothers and sisters from Mexico and Latin America who are being forced by the global economy to leave family and home, risk death in the desert, and work illegally in America. Catholics are faced with this sign even more clearly than most Americans. Just go to Mass in any U.S. city—or many rural parishes, for that matter—and look who is eating with you at the Lord's table. Christ says, "for I was hungry and you gave me food

. . . I was a stranger and you welcomed me" (Matt 25:35). But America calls that "harboring an illegal alien." The signs of the times say it is hard to be Christian in America.

Of course, this is made even more difficult by the fact that America and Christianity are so often equated. The United States Constitution forbids the establishment of any religion, but that has not kept president after president from quoting Christian Scripture, proclaiming America as a "city on a hill," and ending every speech with "God Bless the United States of America." The result has been an unestablished state church of pseudo-Christian civil religion. In his recent book, *The Beloved Community*, Charles Marsh writes that this social reality, particularly in the segregated American South of the mid-twentieth century, "bore striking analogies to fourth-century Christianity after the Edict of Milan in 313 brought an end to Christian persecution and Theodosius I in 380 made the Roman Empire an orthodox Christian state."[4] At precisely that moment in history, Marsh asserts, when church and empire became difficult to differentiate, "men and women were needed who could offer their lives as testimonies to the crucial difference between loyalty to God and loyalty to nation."[5] So, the Desert Fathers and Mothers left the empire's cities and the first monastic movement began. It was when ultimate loyalty became hard to discern that the Spirit began to stir. She stirred again in Saint Benedict to establish the way of life represented here at Saint John's. And she stirred in the twelfth century, at the height of the Crusades, to lead Francis and Dominic into a new form of monasticism. The Bridgefolk[6] group that met here recently has helped me to see that the Anabaptist movement of the sixteenth century was, likewise, a new monastic movement that produced a community of faithful witness at a time of compromise in the church's history. Here, on United States soil, the Spirit stirred again in cotton fields and brush arbors to start a new monastic movement in the slave churches of the South. To this day, members of the black Baptist

---

4. Charles Marsh, *The Beloved Community: How Faith Shapes Social Justice, from the Civil Rights Movement to Today* (New York: Basic Books, 2005), 72.

5. Ibid.

6. For information on Bridgefolk, see their web site: http://bridgefolk.net

church that my wife and I are part of in our neighborhood call one another brother and sister, just as folks do here in the monastery.

As our communities have tried to read the signs of the times and the Spirit's movement in church history, it seems to us that the Spirit is stirring again—stirring to lead us into a new monasticism. We stumbled into this way of life by asking, "What would it mean to pledge our allegiance to God alone?" It seemed to us that God was offering another kingdom, an alternative politics, that is, a whole new way of life for his people in the world. We noted the social relocation associated with monastic movements and said God was calling us to the "abandoned places of empire." We learned about Sabbath, manna, and the Jubilee, and started "sharing economic resources with fellow community members and the needy among us." We considered our adoption as children of God and committed ourselves to "hospitality to the stranger" and "lament for racial division . . . combined with the active pursuit of a just reconciliation." We felt the temptation to think we were doing something radically new and decided instead on "humble submission to Christ's body, the church," maintaining relationships of accountability with local churches. We learned from the monastic practice of a novitiate and have used it to introduce new people to our communities' way of life. We said we would love one another as God has loved us, "nurturing common life among members." When we came together as communities, some of us were married and some of us were single, so we pledged "support for celibate singles alongside monogamous married couples and their children." We are committed to live together and to stick around for the long haul. We noted how connection to place helped us see the need to "care for the plot of God's earth given to us" while also supporting local economies. We felt blessed by God's peace in a violent world and pledged ourselves to "peacemaking in the midst of violence and conflict resolution" among ourselves. We said that all this would only be possible if held together by the "commitment to a disciplined contemplative life."[7] And we prayed that God would lead us, day by day.

7. Quotations in this paragraph are from "12 Marks of a New Monasticism," as articulated by the first New Monasticism Gathering in June of 2004. See Rutba House (ed.), *School(s) for Conversion: 12 Marks of a New Monasticism*, vi.

Perhaps the greatest surprise of this journey has been the response of American Christians. When we published a book of essays on these twelve marks with a little press run by a sister community in Oregon, we hardly expected anyone outside of our communities to read it. Having considered the signs of the times, we had little hope that the American church would take interest. But in the past few years we have been overwhelmed by people saying, "This is just what I've been looking for." *The Christian Century* and *Christianity Today* ran cover stories on new monasticism last fall.[8] When *Time* magazine called in spring 2006 to do a story on what they called this "new movement in American Christianity," I said, "You know we're talking about, at most, a couple thousand people living this way. I mean, most towns have churches bigger than this movement." But new communities are springing up faster than I can keep up with them. It seems that, indeed, the Spirit is stirring.

And I'm reminded once again of old Jonah—how he didn't want to take God's word to the Ninevites, and how, when they heard and repented, he was disappointed by God's mercy. I'm reminded how much bigger God's vision for redemption is than what we can imagine. And I'm excited to be here today with some who've been on the monastic way for centuries and others, like me, who are just getting started. May we, like the good homeowner of Jesus' parable, take from our storage rooms some things old and some things new as we discern how God is leading us to be his people in the world today.

8. Jason Byassee, "The new monastics: Alternative Christian communities," *The Christian Century* 122, no. 21 (October 18, 2005): 38–47; and Rob Moll, "The new monasticism: a fresh crop of Christian communities is blossoming in blighted urban settings all over America," *Christianity Today* 49, no. 9 (September 2005): 38–46.

"Colloquium"

Conversations between
Abbot Primate Notker Wolf, OSB,
and Representatives from Various Communities

*Oblates Reverend Gary Reierson and Shaina M. Crotteau;
Mary David Walgenbach, OSB, of the Benedictine Women of
Madison; Reverend Martin Shannon of the Community of
Jesus; and Jonathan Wilson-Hartgrove of Rutba House;
moderated by Mary Forman, OSB.*

What ascetical practices are necessary for community?

Notker: We need training that becomes second nature to resist temptation with regard to drinking, to other pleasures, or what we would like to do, where a solid structure of the day is already very helpful. As regards eating, we have to stop before we have finished. Some abstinence, like during Lent or on Fridays, helps to assure that we are still free. We have to set up a certain number of rules in a community, like the whole structure, but also privately. We have to encourage people to find their own serious ascetical way in order to respond to their vocation, to the necessity. We need a continuous control as in former times, like the daily examination of our conscience, to overcome our instincts, our impulses, and the ways we get addicted to certain things. Just as those who go into the military undergo a serious training, our aim is not a negativistic attitude for our life in the monastery but to unload many things so as to overcome inertia and to become free.

Jonathan: The thought on fasting, that we give up something in order to fast toward the life of the kingdom, has been important for us. We fast once a week from food, which is a helpful, regular practice. A number of us go to jail for civil disobedience, a kind of asceticism in terms of being bound in order to be free. When we are bound in the prisons for protesting the unjust laws here in the United States, it sets us free to be witnesses in ways we would not be otherwise.

Martin:[1] The Community of Jesus is a mixed community of celibate brothers and sisters and households, and within the household families each home is a multifamily. So, though the celibate brothers and sisters clearly give up marriage and the formal ownership of property, the way we live out that asceticism within the households is that the owner of each home puts the home at the disposal of the community. At times the owners are not living in their own home. Whether we are a nonowner living in someone else's home or not, we agree that part of our ascetic life is periodically to move from place to place. Talk about the inertia—after my wife and I raised four children, we just moved from one home to another; we discovered how much inertia had taken place, even though we said we were not going to accumulate, but we did. Moving overflows into a sense of detachment that all we have is at the disposal of others. This gets very practical when a homeowner watches children from another family break the dishes or glassware or something that is in the home. How we share goods with one another is sacrificial, whether you are a homeowner or one who moves into a home.

---

1. Reverend Martin Shannon is an Episcopal priest who has lived at the Community of Jesus, a Christian community in the Benedictine monastic tradition, based in Orleans, Massachusetts, where he was solemnly professed in 1989. He received an MDiv from Gordon-Conwell Theological Seminary and a PhD in liturgical studies from The Catholic University of America. His doctoral dissertation was on the contribution to the liturgical movement of Damasus Winzen, founder of Mount Saviour Monastery, Elmira, New York. He is married with four grown children and serves his community in the areas of liturgy and formation.

Mary David:[2] The discipline for us is to be available to the many guests at Saint Benedict's—guests at prayer, guests at the meals. So, it is necessary to have that discipline to be available to speak to the guests in such a way that we elicit from them. In our own community we also initiated times of centering prayer together for twenty minutes of silence in the morning and again in the evening. We have also reintroduced time for spiritual reading, which we do as a group, because as a small group in a community we can be very, very busy. So, we have to safeguard those disciplines that help us grow our interior life as well.

Shaina:[3] In living with about two thousand women over at the College of Saint Benedict, one of the practices of being a college oblate is learning how to be constantly with other people. College is very much focused on what needs to be done for classes. But also there is need to take time and attend to my friend. On the flip side, there is also taking the time away from everybody else by taking time for silence because we are constantly going, going, going. So, actually being away from the community to get some private prayer in is very important as well.

Gary:[4] Most ascetical practices are nurtured and sustained by community. As an oblate of Saint John's Abbey, most of my life is not

2. Sister Mary David Walgenbach, OSB, was the prioress of the Sisters of Saint Benedict of Madison, Wisconsin, and cofounder with Sister Joanne Kollasch, OSB, of the Benedictine Women of Madison, an ecumenical Benedictine community in affiliation with the Federation of Saint Gertrude. Mary David spearheaded a long-range environmental and wetland restoration initiative at Saint Benedict Center that has served as a model for local groups and organizations. She has worked in partnership with monasteries in China, Korea, Africa, and the Philippines to improve the lives of women in developing countries and to sponsor several Benedictine women from these countries to gain an education in the United States in colleges and universities. In 2003 she received the Athena Award for helping open doors of leadership opportunity for other women.

3. Shaina M. Crotteau is an oblate of Saint John's Abbey from Orono, Minnesota. She graduated from the College of Saint Benedict, Saint Joseph, Minnesota, in May 2008, having studied theology, psychology, chemistry, biology, piano, and organ. During her college years she pursued a range of activities, from going on mission trips to volunteering in hospice care, teaching ballroom dance to having tea with friends.

4. Reverend Dr. Gary Reierson is president of the Greater Minneapolis Council of Churches, the largest council of churches in the United States and the largest

spent in community, except for the times I am here on retreat. So, a particular challenge for those of us not living in community is to seek to live the Rule in our daily lives.

Martin: In addition, when we talk about community and practicalities, the whole area of indulging in gossip and grumbling comes up. It really is an ascetic exercise to keep one's mouth closed at the proper times. This has been an early rule of our community, which we fail at regularly. Nowadays we have a fancy word for it called triangulation, but back when our community was founded it simply had to do with not talking behind another's back. If there are issues that need to be settled, it can be an ascetic exercise to actually, aggressively, and intentionally go after the resolution of personal differences. It is at the heart of our community's life. While we are not always successful at it, it is an essential ascetic exercise to know when to speak and especially when not to.

Mary: In thinking about ascetical practices as I was studying early monasticism, I was fascinated and touched by Pachomius's model of knowing each of the brothers who came to him in such a way that he assigned a particular mentor to them. Whatever was the vice or struggle of their life and whatever asceticism they would need to practice, they needed to be under the tutelage of someone who knew that the grace of God could work with them in the struggle. In my own life, Sister Annunciata from Switzerland was that for me. As a pharmacist, I would be putting up the meds in the med-room for the sisters to go on their trays in the infirmary, and she would come up to me, look at me and say, "And how is the weather today?" I would say, "I am fine." "The tone of voice is not fine!" she would say. Then we would have a conversation. She was one of my best mentors; she taught me more about authority than any other single person,

volunteer organization in Minnesota, with twenty-seven thousand volunteers. He is nationally recognized for his faith-based initiatives; and he received a three-year federal Compassion Capital Fund intermediary grant to help grassroots groups address human needs in their communities. He received his BA from the University of Minnesota, an MDiv and a doctor of ministry from United Theological Seminary in the Twin Cities. He is the author of *The Art of Preaching* (University Press of America, 1988) and *The Gift of Administration* (Westminster, 1981).

because she loved me out of my rebellious independence, into looking at who the sisters were in the community and how I might approach them.

*In relation to authority, what does it mean to "think with the
community"?*

Notker: As a newly elected abbot, I never liked to hurt people
or to be too harsh. But later on I realized that if I don't stop a confrere
from doing this or that, I am unjust to the whole community. So, for
the sake of others, I have to be very clear, outspoken, but not be
harsh; perhaps for the other one it sounds harsh. Later on, especially
when I visited a sick brother who opened up completely his whole
life, I learned to see my brothers from the side of God. God has created them and continues to love them. Once we look into the life of
a brother or sister, it is a miracle to see how God is working. We
respect them in a different way. If we are in a dialogue with our
brother or our sister, then we can tell them uneasy things and explain
them in a different way.

Mary David: The way I would help the individual is to invite
them to offer their own lives and then to put emphasis on how we
as a community help one another to do that, not only by having
skills and workshops available to learn and use the skills, but also
we do that through the daily chapter meeting. I firmly believe that
self-development is extremely important in order to be obedient. I need
to know who I am and how I offer my life in order to give it up. That is
an attitude we can have in the community that we try to practice together. Then community participation can be very open and honest.

Jonathan: Our community practices decision-making by con-
sensus, so we have a regular practice of listening to one another. Also,
we try to practice what Jesus says in Matthew 18: that if someone
sins against you, you go to talk to them directly. We always try to
submit ourselves to the authority of one another. In that process one
of the things that I have learned is the authority that love produces.
It is a lot easier to hear from some people than from others. I have

noticed that the people I can hear are the people I know love me. They usually do a lot of stuff to love me and serve me and in the midst of it, as casually as we might talk about the weather, they say something like, "Maybe you should think about this. It could be sin."

Gary: Oblates do not "think with the community" very often, except perhaps for the small portions of time we are on retreat, although there is a kind of thinking with the community that has just recently been launched. The oblates of this abbey are very well aware of what we have received from the abbey in terms of our own deepened spiritual lives. The "thinking with the community" that has just begun, and Abbot John is very open to the conversation, is what are the gifts and graces that we can bring not only to the monastic community but also in outreach in the world, which becomes increasingly relevant as the monastic community is growing smaller and as the oblates are growing. We have not yet had that kind of conversation, but it is a strategic moment when that conversation will increasingly take place. It will require some give-and-take between the oblates and the monastic community, who perhaps have not thought about us precisely in this way in the past.

Martin: Your story of your mentor reminded me of an assistance in learning to think communally rather than just individually and rather than just authoritatively, so to speak. When I moved to the Community of Jesus, I had been in pastoral ministry for eleven years and was doing ongoing theological work. With all sorts of things to offer and readiness to offer them, I was assigned to work with an older pastor whom I had known for a number of years and was very close to. The way he got me thinking along with the community was by the regular use of the word, "no." I worked on the staff with him in pastoral care within the community and he said, "Just bring your ideas to me any time." For the first eight months or so, I just knew that the answer was going to be "no." I'd bring my ideas and he would say, "No . . . no . . . no," so much so, I'd get mad and we'd work it through; nothing would come of it, and my idea was turned down. Anyway, after about eight months, I went his office with some idea that I no longer remember what it was, but I do remember the specific time, and he said, "That's a good idea and we'll do that." I shook in my boots. It frightened me. "Now he is actually going to listen." I said to him, "What's the difference? You were saying 'no' for so long, and I don't know if what I suggested is all that different." He said, "Up until now your ideas have mostly been put forth for the sake of putting forth your ideas, which is fine. I don't want not to affirm your thinking, but you're not thinking about the community and what's best for the whole community. That's not your motivation." It seemed harsh at the time. I don't know that he said "yes" to everything after that, but I got very careful about what I was bringing to him because I realized he really was listening, but it was a process for me to begin thinking beyond the scope of my own strengths or gifts, to thinking about service to the community. Thinking with one another has to do with what our motivations are.

How have any of you responded to accusations of belonging to a cult?

Martin: In the early days of the Community of Jesus, which was founded in the 1960s and 1970s, it was a pretty rigid organization. Unfortunately, there were a lot of charismatic groups coming out at that time. Our relationship with the larger town of Orleans was not all that great. It is totally different now. The attempt to try to mold an intentional community, which took its Christianity seriously but was not following any of the particular models in this small town of New England, was looked upon with a fair amount of suspicion. Now the townspeople view us with a great deal of pride and suggest that the tour buses on the route for Cape Cod Tours stop at the community church. So, things have changed. I was not in the community at that time but I've heard stories of that kind of thinking. The community began about the same period as Jonestown, as a group that was tightly knit and not in communication with the larger town. We may have deserved some of the suspicion that came our way. Since then we have some people serving on town boards. In those founding years some mistakes were made in terms of communication with the larger community. But since then we have survived the founding.

Shaina: I have actually had Protestant friends come up to me and looked at Catholicism as a whole as some kind of strange cult. It sounds funny, especially since there are two billion Christians on the planet. It is a matter of recognizing where somebody else is at and that their tradition may have said something poorly about yours and being hospitable toward them and explaining respectfully without being angry.

Jonathan: The only thing that I would add is: transparency helps folks to get over fears. When people ask if we might be part of a cult, there is a fear of something that is true, which is that "cult" is very close to culture. A people might have a culture or whole way of life that they are living out together that is a counterculture to the culture at large, and so it seems dangerous to some folks. There is some truth to that. It seems to me that Jesus started the greatest counterculture that has ever been and we're called into that. To be the people of God in the world is to be a peculiar people, so if some folks continue to look at us strangely it might be just part of the nature of following Jesus.

What are the challenges of formation for newer as well as older foundations and as oblates?

Jonathan: Our community has tried to learn from the Benedictines. We have something like a novitiate, a year during which a mentor from the community meets regularly with new folks. This book on the twelve marks of a new monasticism has theological reflection on each of those practices. So, in our formation process we work through those over the course of the year.

Mary David: We are a new noncanonical community backing off from the old canonical way, so our challenge is that, as Protestant women come to our place, we need to have an ecumenical formation, so that we can appreciate each other's denomination and approach to living and praying together. We do some history and some worship rites; we talk about what was lost in each of our denominations; and then, of course, there is the whole monastic formation, in which we pretty much follow the Benedictine tradition.

Shaina: For college oblates we utilize all the resources on campus, but also we recognize that we are not going to be here on campus our entire lives. We must make sure we ground ourselves here and also live out the lifestyle with the community when we live very far away.

Gary: The oblate program here at Saint John's is very flexible and very open mostly because the oblates come from a variety of different circumstances and geographic locations. So, people make of the oblate program what they will. While that is a great joy for those of us who are oblates, it is also marked by a freedom of individual expression that means that we are not all formed in a similar fashion, which makes it harder for us as a group to coalesce even when we are here in community for a period of time.

Martin: Our community is at the stage of life where we have moved away from the founding generation, attempting to institutionalize ourselves in the best sense of the word. We come to Benedictines because they have been at it so long; it's a challenging process to pass on a charism that really goes on from person to person, not just from mind to mind. How do we keep the original charism alive and do so in a way that provides some structure and thinking? We also have the added challenge of formation not just of the new members who come without knowing the Community of Jesus at all, but we have children who grow up in community: how do they discern whether or not they are called to live there? So, we are beginning to formalize a process of formation just in the last couple of years to address both of those areas. So, I am open to anybody who has brilliant ideas of how you take a charism and embody it. We think it happens through people more than through words, that is, with living in the home as well as some study, but mostly through the relationships and periods of time.

Notker: The Congregation for Religious in Rome never understands that a monastic community is like a family. It develops over time and later on the community lives on in its own story, which gives the identity to the community. The novitiate means that the community introduces somebody into the life and the story of a family, of a community, which can only be done through persons, as

Martin said. Looking back when members are growing older, it is not what they learned in the novitiate but certain members of the community who shaped and formed them. While intellectual input, say from the internet, is important, the internet can never replace a person. Formation is of the whole man or woman, slowly growing in a continuous transformation. Even elder monks still have to learn what it means to become older; in this regard one has a good tradition where a monk or nun introduces to another monk or nun, person to person.

Jonathan: Abbot Wolf, is there monastic wisdom for how to start a new community?

Notker: Ja. Maybe not wisdom, as some experience. When I was archabbot of Sankt Ottilien, we started a number of new communities. At least two or three people, maybe more, are needed to begin, but they need to be strong characters who can live together and have gotten to know each other so they are bound together. They need to be enough to manage so many things—offices, bureaucracy—and to pray together, even if one of them is gone. They need to be deeply rooted spiritually and flexible in their imagination, because even if they start with a certain program, they will have to rewrite it. Nevertheless, they need a basic vision they want to accomplish in order to inspire some other people. Then at a certain point the devil will creep in because he cannot allow the growing of a new place of adoration of God. Usually he starts with the relationship between two or three people. Or with monks, during this period of frustration, some woman enters. During a tough time the most important things are sincerity, faithfulness, strength of character, and a deep prayer life. Also in the beginning a means of selection is needed; our discernment has to be rather tough with candidates. Strong characters keep the community from falling apart; later on, when the community is larger, it can carry on its shoulders weaker characters. It is important that the founding members feel the love and concern of the founding community, especially of the leader, who goes there to encourage them, to be present, and so they don't feel alone. It is challenging but very rewarding and enjoyable to start a new community.

Mary David: In addition, a new community must keep its eye on the vision and find allies who also believe in the vision even if outside the particular community.

What rites of passage does the community have to become part of it?

Jonathan: For our community, because of hospitality there are guests who have become members, so that transition is important to name. Our community has developed a rule of life that we actually call "our road together" by which we agree to live together as a way to live to freedom. We name commitments and have a covenant retreat each year where we recommit and look again at our covenant, if we need to rephrase anything.

Martin: Early on in the life of our community, a small group of single women, who became the actual core of our current sisterhood, wanted vows. That eventually developed into our "rule of life," which provides for the novitiate for the brotherhood/sisterhood, and for the household—the large community as well; and a simple profession renewed every year; and then solemn profession, which includes a profession of stability to live out our days at Rock Harbor, Massachusetts. Those vows are made in the context of liturgy once a year. The brothers and sisters all have habits; the rest of us have an alb, a baptismal garment. We wear those to our Offices as a sign of our common life and our vows. When we make simple profession, we receive that robe. When we make solemn profession, we receive a scapular that goes with the robe. There are ways that we are known by sight as well.

Notker: One problem to be faced is that the longer a community is living together, the more its language becomes a common language, but the danger is in becoming a ghetto for newcomers. They have to take up the language of this community. Continuous contact with guests and listening to them can bring some good new input. Also chapter 3 of the Rule of Benedict says that for important questions the abbot should convoke the whole community because God oftentimes tells the youngest one what is better. A community has to work against the danger of becoming a ghetto.

What advice would you give to a new community for the transition into the second or third generation?

Martin: There is a degree of faithfulness to the vision that has to be maintained; that is done through persons clearly. There is just dogged determination to maintain certain values that you started with and won't give up on. The larger a community gets, you begin to lose some of those initial values. There has to be a degree of adaptability, so how do you maintain those values when the guesthouse and liturgies are always full of guests? The third thing is that you have to know the questions to ask, which you discover as you go along. I don't know if there is a fail-safe method of making that transition. Part of the reason why we wrote a rule of life is that we are convinced that the day will come when our community will need reform. It can look to the rule to do that. So, there is no advice; there's just more questions to answer.

Section II

Monastic Practices

"Promises make an uncertain future more predictable; when kept, in addition to fostering trust, they give a certain steadiness to our purposes. They allow for dependability in relationships, even when encountering trouble spots. They are deeply connected to our ability to sustain hope. Promises safeguard us against our own inconsistencies and fickleness and give stability to our love."

— Christine Pohl,
paraphrasing Lewis B. Smedes and Margaret A. Farley

Practices at the Heart
of Community Life*

Christine D. Pohl[1]

Introduction

Most people long to experience the kind of communities that are loving, grace filled, life-giving, and good. People yearn for settings in which they can move toward wholeness while simultaneously sharing their gifts with others. Christians of all sorts desire communities that capture the beauty of life as God intended it. And communities—whether monastic, intentional, familial, or congregational—are places of deepest fulfillment and, at times, of profound disappointment. Failed experiments in community litter the Christian landscape, but people who have experienced vibrant, loving community know that it is a dimension of what human beings were made for.

* Some of the views in this essay will appear in greatly expanded form in a book by Christine Pohl on the practices of community, to be published by the William B. Eerdmans Publishing Company. We are grateful to Eerdmans for permission to publish this essay.

1. Christine Pohl is professor of church in society at Asbury Theological Seminary in Wilmore, Kentucky, a seminary in the Wesleyan Holiness tradition. She is author of *Making Room: Recovering Hospitality as a Christian Tradition* (Grand Rapids, MI: Wm. B. Eerdmans, 1999), which was written during her sabbatical at the Collegeville Institute. She also serves on the board of the Louisville Institute.

My interest in understanding better the practices that are at the heart of community life emerged gradually from working on a single practice—hospitality. Part of my research for the book *Making Room* involved visiting eight intentional Christian communities whose life together centered around substantial welcoming of strangers. To learn more about contemporary challenges facing practitioners of hospitality, I spent time at L'Arche, the Catholic Worker, Open Door, L'Abri, and Benedictine communities. I participated in their shared life, interviewed hosts and guests, studied their publications, and observed interactions.

The insights I gained from these visits were profoundly formative for how I have understood the ways in which hospitality can be recovered for our life today. Issues that are faced in intentional communities—concerns about the relationship between communal identity and welcoming people from different backgrounds, holding in tension fidelity and personal freedom, the rhythms of work and rest, limits and abundance, grace and responsibility—are faced by every sort of community. But when people live in close proximity, have articulated shared commitments, and have identified common tasks or ministry, the issues are often posed more quickly and acutely than in ordinary church life. Intentional communities provide insight into the complexity and importance of practices for all sorts of human relationships and connections.

Challenges of Sustaining Communities of Welcome

In interviews with practitioners who offer daily welcome to strangers, I asked about the challenges and blessings of their work. I was surprised by the number who said to me, "you can't offer any sustained hospitality to strangers apart from a strong community" but then they followed that insight by saying, "sustaining community is so much more difficult than welcoming strangers." These comments helped to launch my present research.[2]

2. Part of my current research was funded by the Lilly Endowment's "Sustaining Pastoral Excellence" Initiative. The "Pastor in Community" project provided excep-

And so, on the one hand, there is an unfocused, societal-wide yearning for community and, on the other, a truthful recognition of its challenges by persons who have chosen that life. Contemporary as well as biblical emphases on the centrality of community to Christian identity are accompanied by a number of powerful social, economic, and ecclesial factors that discourage attempts at a richer communal life. All of this suggests that the contemporary church might benefit from teasing out some of the practices that make community life possible. What is it that faithful people have done together, over the centuries and in light of God's word and work, that has made life together possible and good?[3]

Much is at stake. A number of contemporary Christian writers and academics are emphasizing the significance and role of Christian community. In ethics, theology, and biblical studies, there is fresh attention to what it means to be the people of God, to recovering the social dimensions of the kingdom, and to practicing the new community of the church.[4]

In his book *Ancient-Future Faith* Robert Webber argues that if the church of the twenty-first century is to be and to bring Good News to the world, local churches will need to embody a winsome communal life. With some optimism, he writes about the apologetic significance and impact of Christian community. "The church is the primary presence of God's activity in the world. As we pay attention to what it means to be the church we create an alternative community

---

tional opportunities to study practices in relation to community and congregational life. This chapter is a summary of some of the fruits of that study. My more complete study of practices in relation to community life will be available in book form from Wm. B. Eerdmans Publishing Company in the next year.

3. This question is only a slight modification of the definition of practices offered by Dorothy Bass and Craig Dykstra in *Practicing Theology*. In their essay on "A Theological Understanding of Practices," Bass and Dykstra describe "Christian practices" as "things Christian people do together over time to address fundamental human needs in response to and in the light of God's active presence for the life of the world." Their understanding of practices is indebted to the work of Alasdair MacIntyre, and I have found this understanding of practices to be particularly helpful. Miroslav Volf and Dorothy C. Bass, eds., *Practicing Theology: Beliefs and Practices in Christian Life* (Grand Rapids, MI: Wm. B. Eerdmans, 2002), 18.

4. See, for example, the work of N. T. Wright and Stanley Hauerwas.

to the society of the world. This new community, the embodied experience of God's kingdom, will draw people into itself and nurture them in the faith. In this sense the church and its life in the world will become the new apologetic. People come to faith not because they see the logic of the argument, but because they have experienced a welcoming God in a hospitable and loving community."[5]

Similarly, Jean Vanier concludes his book *Community and Growth* with the observation that, given the deep loneliness of many people today and their yearning for belonging and meaning, what is needed is "many small communities which will welcome lost and lonely people, offering them a new form of family and a sense of belonging." He continues, "In the past, Christians who wanted to follow Jesus opened hospitals and schools. Now that there are so many of these, Christians must commit themselves to the new communities of welcome."[6]

At the end of *After Virtue*, Alasdair MacIntyre's call for a new Saint Benedict and for newly created local communities is surprisingly comprehensive in its expectation that such forms of communal life are crucial to the future of humanity in the West.[7] Similarly, Jonathan Wilson's suggestion for a "new monasticism" in which the Gospel is embodied in numerous small communities of faith echoes a renewed interest in recovering communal aspects of the Christian tradition that have been eclipsed in recent centuries.[8]

A vibrant Christian community is the most important apologetic for the Gospel—it always has been. Jesus' prayer in John 17:20-26 that the oneness and love among the Godhead would be lived out and experienced among believers—so that the world would believe that Jesus had been sent by God—is an extraordinary testimony to the importance of our shared life. Love within community, flowing

5. Robert E. Webber, *Ancient-Future Faith* (Grand Rapids, MI: Baker, 1999), 72.

6. Jean Vanier, *Community and Growth*, rev. ed. (New York: Paulist Press, 1989), 283.

7. Alasdair MacIntyre, *After Virtue* (Notre Dame, IN: University of Notre Dame Press, 1984), 263.

8. Jonathan R. Wilson, *Living Faithfully in a Fragmented World* (Harrisburg, PA: Trinity Press International, 1997).

from the love and communion of the Trinity, is evidence of the truth of the Gospel and of Christian discipleship (see also John 13:34-35). Forming and sustaining such communities, however, has never been easy. The difficulty is compounded today because, while Christians may want a richer experience of community, many have been shaped by an individualistic, therapeutic, and market-oriented culture.

The result, at the popular level especially, is that even when thinking about community and relationships, contemporary followers of Jesus are more comfortable with therapeutic language and business models than they are with theological categories. Congregations and pastors are as inclined to look to the best-selling management book as they are to reflect theologically on congregational visions or differences. Similarly, in addressing relational difficulties, Christians are as likely to talk about dysfunctional personalities and addictive behavior as to speak in terms of fidelity, gratitude, or sin. While resources from the fields of business and psychology are certainly helpful, they are not adequate, and the church has largely lost hold of its own language that is far richer for questions of life in community.

People turn toward Christian communities with hope and longing for close, transparent relationships, a deeper spiritual life, and a more responsible use of resources. Disappointment—with shallow spirituality, materialism, consumption, restless striving, disregard for creation, divisions between rich and poor people, and a lack of time for relationships—pushes persons toward community but does not equip them for it. Dissatisfaction with life as it is lived presently does not, in itself, prepare people for new forms of community.

Whether considering joining a monastic community, becoming a member of a church congregation, or starting a marriage, many in our culture bring with them a wariness of commitments and a reluctance to foreclose personal options. They are often deeply uncertain about limits, boundaries, authority, and rules. Cultural emphases on self-actualization, entitlement, individual rights, and autonomy make life together a challenge, whatever the nature of the community.

So, if the yearnings for community and the recent appreciation for its importance to Christian life and identity are not just an optimistic grasping for the next cultural or ecclesial fix, then it is important that we look more closely at what sustains life together and at what breaks it apart.

Practices at the Heart of Community Life

There are many ways to anchor a discussion of the practices at the heart of community life, but a particularly compelling one emerges from the picture of Jesus in the first chapter of John's gospel. Jesus who "became flesh and lived among us" is described as "full of grace and truth." "From his fullness," John says, "we have all received, grace upon grace" (John 1:14-16). Communities anchored in Christ are enabled to reflect and to draw from his grace and truth. But what do grace and truth look like within human relationships, or said slightly differently, what are the relational dynamics of grace and truth? How might Christians cultivate a culture of grace and truth in our communities, families, churches, and schools?[9]

In truth-shaped and grace-filled communities, people keep their promises; they live truthfully; they live gratefully and hospitably. Promise keeping, truthfulness, gratitude, and hospitality are not the only practices necessary for communities to flourish—there are other central practices like forgiveness, discernment, worship, prayer, and keeping Sabbath—but these four are central to cultivating a good life together.[10]

Despite the importance of these practices, we often find it easier to see their deformations—in the form of betrayal, deception, envy or grumbling, and exclusion. Unless the circumstances are unusual, we tend not to notice when promise keeping and truth telling are operating well. They are like the beams of a house—ignored unless they are disintegrating and the roof sags or the ceiling collapses.[11]

9. Chris P. Rice writes powerfully about creating a "culture of grace" in his book *Grace Matters* (San Francisco, CA: Jossey-Bass, 2002), 259–61.

10. The choice to focus on these four practices emerged from the concerns I encountered in communities of hospitality, along with the recognition that promise keeping, truthfulness, and gratitude have received little attention in the current literature on practices (though they were central in the ethics literature of the past).

11. Stephen V. Doughty, *Discovering Community* (Nashville, TN: Upper Room, 1999), 136–37.

However, if we are not attentive to the importance of keeping promises and living truthfully, we're unlikely to be able to stand against the powerful contemporary assault on these practices. In a culture that expects "spin" and celebrates self-actualization, concerns about fidelity and truthfulness can seem quite outdated and naïve. But no community can survive without them and many have been undermined by small infidelities and deceptions.

Neither can a community survive without practicing gratitude and hospitality. Communities collapse under the weight of grumbling and dissatisfaction, envy and presumption. Whether among the children of Israel in the desert or folks in a local church, grumbling and ingratitude are community killers. Once under way, they are almost impossible to address and they slowly drain the life and joy out of relationships. Communities that have trouble making room for strangers because they have grown so insulated or so preoccupied with their own needs or struggles are communities that are dying.[12] When there is little room for strangers, there's also increasingly little room for members.

Each of these practices has a significant theological and philosophical literature associated with it, has rich resonance in the biblical and historical tradition, and is practically necessary to the Christian life. Vulnerable to contemporary cultural values and social pressures, as well as to human sin and finitude, each practice can also be readily undermined. In the remainder of this essay, a closer look at each of the four practices will be provided.

Gratitude

At the heart of the Christian life is gratitude; it is the fitting response to viewing our lives as defined by costly grace. "[T]hanksgiving is what characterizes 'God's holy people' (Eph 5:3, 1 Thess 4:3-8),"[13]

---

12. Vanier, *Community and Growth*, 267.

13. David W. Pao, *Thanksgiving: An Investigation of a Pauline Theme*, New Testament Studies in Biblical Theology 13 (Downers Grove, IL: InterVarsity Press, 2002), 96.

"and failure to give thanks to God is idolatry."[14] In Romans 1, Paul asserts that at the root of human sin is the refusal to trust and to honor God and a failure to give God thanks. In his discussion of this passage, Martin Luther suggests that ingratitude is the root of all evil.[15] "It is how sin takes shape within us . . . and holds us captive."[16]

Because of God's grace, the most fitting posture in entering any sort of community is "not as demanders but as thankful recipients." Dietrich Bonhoeffer has written that because God has laid the foundation and has brought us together in Christ, our communal life should be shaped by gratitude.[17] The more thankfully we receive what has been given to us, the stronger and deeper our community grows.

It may be helpful to think about gratitude at multiple levels: to God, as a posture for life, and to one another. When gratitude characterizes both a communal life and the individual lives of the persons in community, it is often accompanied by contentment. Persons have a sense of being blessed and are eager to confer blessing; they are attentive to the goodness and beauty in everyday things. In a culture of grace and gratitude, persons and their contributions are acknowledged and honored, and there is regular testimony to God's faithfulness through which community members experience one another's joys. Expressions of gratitude help make the community alive to the Word, the Spirit, and to God's work.

Gratitude can be distorted by an expectation that somehow Christians are always supposed to be smiling and cheerful, even in the face of suffering, tragedy, or grave injustice. It is deformed by the notion that living gratefully involves denying the misery and evil around us. Sometimes people and communities demand gratitude and turn its importance into a spiritual bludgeon used to smash the heartache or experiences of betrayal out of people so they can quickly be moved into a more cheerful state that is so much more bearable for everyone around them.

14. Ibid., 157. In a number of philosophical traditions, gratitude is viewed as the greatest of the virtues.

15. Ibid., 162, quoting Martin Luther (*Luther's Works*, 1959:26).

16. Mary Jo Leddy, *Radical Gratitude* (Maryknoll, NY: Orbis, 2002), 61.

17. Dietrich Bonhoeffer, *Life Together* (HarperSanFrancisco, 1954), 28.

Gratitude involves knowing that we are held secure by a loving God, and that ultimately the God we worship is trustworthy and good, despite the nearly unbearable sorrow that might be encountered along the way. It is acknowledging that we do not always know the whole story, and that we are living before it is finished, and that we are thankful for the presence of God and faithful persons in our lives. Gratitude is a crucial way in which death and destruction do not have the final word and cannot finally define us.[18]

Simple words of thanks and acknowledgment can bestow surprising blessing. A pastor and cofounder of an intentional community in Cincinnati has reflected deeply on the significance of gratitude and tells stories of how moments of affirmation and gratitude in his church have been life-giving. He describes simple rituals of blessing that acknowledge what a person means to others—before they are dead and the words are delivered as a eulogy. He notes that after one of these times of deliberate blessing among the leadership team of his church, he was reduced to tears for hours because of the deep encouragement it represented. He writes:

> Gratitude and affirmation are in short supply. Sadly, I must admit that I'm not only ingratitude's victim, but also its perpetrator. Often I have shrugged off gratitude while embracing discontent. Usually I can justify this in the name of 'vision' or 'unmet potential.' That is until I read the following quote from Dietrich Bonhoeffer [in *Life Together*, p. 29; see note 19]:

> "We think we dare not be satisfied with the small measure of spiritual knowledge, experience, and love that has been given to us, and that we must constantly be looking forward eagerly for the highest good . . . we pray for the big things and forget to give thanks for the ordinary, small (and yet really not small) gifts. How can God entrust great things to one who will not thankfully receive from Him the little things? If we do not give thanks daily for the Christian fellowship in which we have been placed, even when there is no great experience, no discoverable riches, but much weakness, small faith, and difficulty; if on the contrary, we only keep complaining to God

18. Leddy, *Radical Gratitude*, 51.

that everything is so paltry and petty, so far from what we expected, then we hinder God from letting our fellowship grow according to the measure and riches which are there for us all in Jesus Christ."

The pastor continues,

I can only imagine if this advice were heeded by even a fraction of a local church—the effects could be revolutionary. How many times have I wished I were somewhere else where God was REALLY moving? How many times have I longed to be in a more beautiful place (with mountains or an ocean) and abandon the urban neighborhood where I live? How many times have I fantasized about the perfect fellowship where everyone got along like a perfect family. . . . It's poison . . . Thankfully the antidote is available and accessible: equal parts of gratitude and affirmation.[19]

Challenges to Cultivating Gratitude

These insights are valuable reminders that gratitude can be undone in subtle ways. When we yearn for some ideal of church or community, it is easy to become deeply dissatisfied with what we have. While we might readily acknowledge that always wanting more possessions or money is wrong, sometimes we overlook the danger of always wanting more success in our ministries, greater spiritual growth in ourselves or others, or more dramatic spiritual experiences. Always wanting more good things can be unhelpful; nevertheless, it can be difficult to live in the tension between being grateful for what we have been given and striving for excellence and growth. Given our cultural emphases on growth and success, however, gratitude is often overlooked and contentment is misinterpreted as an absence of drive or vision.

Efforts to cultivate a practice and posture of gratitude will encounter other challenges. Strong notions of entitlement undermine any sense of ourselves as receivers of gifts. Paul Tournier has observed that "no gift can bring joy to the one who has a right to every-

---

19. Kevin Rains, Vineyard Central Church, Cincinnati, Ohio. Quote used by permission.

thing."[20] If we are entitled to everything, we end up thankful for nothing.[21] While there is a healthy notion of entitlement that is tied to a sense of personhood, dignity, and equality, when it is exaggerated, it brings continual dissatisfaction and the incapacity to appreciate anything as a gift.

Another challenge to gratitude is grumbling. Within communities, grumbling is highly contagious and occasional complaining and dissatisfaction can become a way of life. In C. S. Lewis's words, people can go from grumbling to becoming "a grumble," a very deadly condition.[22] The Rule of Benedict appears to take grumbling quite seriously; it is clearly understood as a threat to communal life and goodness (see RB 4.39; 5.14-19; 23.1; 34.3-7; 40.8-9).[23] While the Rule warns regularly about those who grumble, it also shows sensitivity to circumstances that can cause unnecessary hardship. For example, kitchen workers are to be provided with special food and help so their service to the community and to guests can be "without grumbling." Decisions made by leaders are to allow for a life in which community members can "go about their activities without justifiable grumbling" (RB 35.12-13; 53.18; 41.5). Interestingly, the Rule thus allows some category of "justifiable grumbling" (41.5) and suggests that expectations of gratitude can foreclose justifiable criticism or can misinterpret truth telling as grumbling. When an unwelcome truth about injustice or irresponsibility is spoken, it is easy for those with institutional power to dismiss it wrongly as ingratitude. In the Rule, the antidote to grumbling seems to be a combination of humility, contentment, and gratitude.

Gratitude is thus central to life in community; without it fidelity and hospitality quickly become burdensome and truthfulness can

---

20. Quoted in Paul F. Camenisch, "Gift and Gratitude in Ethics," *Journal of Religious Ethics*, no. 9 (Spring 1981): 23.

21. "Gratitude" in Christopher Peterson and Martin E. P. Seligman, *Character Strengths and Virtues* (New York: Oxford University Press, 2004), 564.

22. C. S. Lewis, *The Great Divorce* (New York: HarperCollins, 1946, 2001), 75–78.

23. Timothy Fry, ed., *Rule of St. Benedict 1980* (Collegeville, MN: Liturgical Press, 1981).

be harsh and cold. Gratitude helps us see what is good, and it sustains the other practices.[24]

Promise Keeping or Fidelity

No community endures without trust that is based in fidelity. "Life together survives . . . not on a steady diet of warm feelings but on the tough fibers of promise keeping," as Lewis Smedes has observed.[25] Promise making and promise keeping, the structures of fidelity, are at the root of our ability to trust one another, and without some measure of trust, it is difficult to do almost anything.

The context of our promise making and keeping is God's love, integrity, and faithfulness.[26] In Psalm 33:4-5 we read that all God's work is done in faithfulness and "the earth is full of the steadfast love of the Lord." Making and keeping promises are central aspects of our relationship with God, of God's relationship with us, and of our relationships with one another.

Characteristics of contemporary culture make fidelity or promise keeping in the context of community very uncertain. Today we are jaded about promises, partly as a result of the continual hype of advertising that makes promises about products none of us believes. Whether about diet plans, new cars, detergents, or running shoes, the promises are often quite incredible. Additionally, we are profoundly skeptical of politicians who make impossible promises to whatever constituency they are currently courting. We are very familiar with a

24. In practicing gratitude, there are additional complexities. Sometimes we are challenged by being given gifts we do not want and sacrifices we did not ask for. Gifts create a moral tie between giver and recipient that is sometimes desirable but in other cases problematic. Even in grateful communities, it is not always easy to know how and where to acknowledge people's contributions, especially the quiet, undramatic gifts that are not readily noticeable.

25. Lewis B. Smedes, "Controlling the Unpredictable: The Power of Promising." *Christianity Today* (January 21, 1983): 19.

26. Examples of the centrality of fidelity in the Scriptures include Psalm 25:10: "All the paths of the LORD are steadfast love and faithfulness, for those who keep his covenant and his decrees." In 2 Peter, Jesus' followers are described as living in and by the promises of Christ. In 2 Corinthians 1:20, Paul says that in Jesus, "every one of God's promises is a 'Yes.'"

complicated legal system that makes sure that individuals and companies both keep their promises and have ways to get out of them—whether marriage vows or refrigerator warrantees.

Despite the current level of cynicism about fidelity, many people continue to make and to keep promises. Lewis Smedes notes, people "choose not to quit when the going gets rough because they promised once to see it through. They stick to lost causes. They hold on to a love grown cold. They stay with people who have become pains in the neck. They still dare to make promises and care enough to keep the promises they make." Smedes continues, "if you have a ship you will not desert, if you have people you will not forsake, if you have causes you will not abandon, then *you are like God*."[27] His claim is startling, but the God we worship is one who has made promises to us and lives in covenant with us.

Promises make an uncertain future more predictable; when kept, in addition to fostering trust, they give a certain steadiness to our purposes. They allow for dependability in relationships even when encountering trouble spots. They are deeply connected to our ability to sustain hope. Promises safeguard us against our own inconsistencies and fickleness and give stability to our love.[28]

Promises take many forms; some are formal, such as vows, oaths, or covenants. We make promises upon entrance into a marriage, baptism, ordination, or a monastic community. Other promises are informal, the stuff of every day life—we'll be there at ten, I'll cook on Wednesday. There are explicit promises, ones we articulate to others, and many that are implicit, unarticulated, but they nevertheless set up expectations. Often the expectations are fairly ordinary, but people arrange their behavior and choices based on these expectations. If promises fail or if they are not kept, experiences of betrayal and disappointment can sometimes be acute.

27. Lewis B. Smedes, "The Power of Promises," in *A Chorus of Witnesses*, ed. Thomas G. Long and Cornelius Plantinga Jr. (Grand Rapids, MI: Wm. B. Eerdmans, 1994), 156.

28. Ibid., 158. See also Margaret A. Farley, *Personal Commitments* (San Francisco, CA: Harper & Row, 1986), 19–20, 34–35, 39.

We are most likely to run into misunderstandings and disappointments in the area of implicit promises. When expectations have not been spelled out, people may have very different assumptions without even realizing it. Particularly in times of transition, and when communities are incorporating new people or new leadership, it is helpful to be clear about expectations and commitments.

Challenges to Fidelity

The Christian faith is rooted in promises and yet Christians struggle with the practice of fidelity for a number of reasons. In a culture that celebrates the notion of unlimited choice, we often want to keep our options open. Making promises and commitments foreclose some good opportunities. Knowing that some change in circumstances is inevitable, we are afraid to make commitments that bind us to a particular future. Life together can be quite fragile when the fear of foreclosing options combines with a perpetual dissatisfaction or yearning for more and better spiritual or communal experiences.

We do not make or keep promises in a vacuum. Particular promises are always made in the midst of other commitments, and so we struggle with conflicting commitments, frailty, and finitude. Philosophers write about "conditions that defeat a promise"—the reasons promises might fail. Not all conflicts run so deep that they endanger the relationship or the community, but sometimes they do, and forgiveness is often necessary.

Betrayals or deliberate violations of fidelity are often dependent on deception and secrecy, connecting promise keeping and truthfulness at a deep level. Experiences of betrayal are devastating to persons and communities. Unfortunately, the Gospel does not suggest that a life of faithfulness, love, and service will be protected from disappointments, betrayals, and failure. In the cross, however, we witness both the bearing of deep betrayals and the assurance that it is possible, by grace and forgiveness, to redeem broken promises and to recover from failures in commitments.

Cultivating a culture of fidelity involves recognition of its costliness and readiness to honor the sacrifices it sometimes involves.

Small acts of fidelity, presence, and promise keeping add up to a way of life that is holy and winsome. Historic monasticism, especially Benedictine communities, has understood the significance of stability and of commitment to a place. Such commitments are profoundly countercultural, and yet at the same time they speak to a contemporary hunger for place, tradition, and community. Commitments to forgotten neighborhoods and marginalized groups of people also characterize many of the new intentional communities, revealing the importance of fidelity within communities and also to the larger community.

In writing about healthy communities, Jean Vanier has observed that their "essential nourishment is fidelity to the thousand and one small demands of each day."[29] Despite the cost involved, promise making and promise keeping are fundamentally nourishing and life-giving.

Truth Telling or Truthfulness

Like promise keeping, truth telling is a practice we tend to overlook unless it fails. While it is impossible to sustain a life together without a commitment to living truthfully with one another, today we might be quite inclined to echo the Old Testament lament that truth has fallen in the streets, and that people rely on empty arguments and speak lies, driving justice, righteousness, and honesty far away. Whether exhibited by petty criminals or by well-placed corporate executives, pastors, priests, doctors, or political leaders, deception, dishonesty, and exaggeration are part of the contemporary landscape. The resultant cynicism and doubt about truthfulness in business, government, the military, and religious institutions runs deep.

Within the philosophical and theological literatures, there is significant discussion about truth telling and whether it is ever right to lie. However, I have found a more fruitful approach involves focusing on what it means to be a truthful community. What does a community look like that loves the truth or that lives truthfully?

29. Vanier, *Community and Growth*, 169.

In truthful communities members are able to avoid posturing; they do not need to keep up appearances or pretend that everything is good when it is not. They attend to details and do not close their eyes to difficulties. People who love the truth name deception and dissimulation early and call things "by their proper names."[30] They have an accurate sense of their own fallenness and of God's truth and goodness. In such communities people take responsibility for their mistakes and for their sin.

In truthful communities we find a close correspondence between what people say and what they do, a well-developed capacity to listen to one another, and with that, a posture of receptiveness, hospitality, and discernment. As noted in James 1:19, such communities help their members learn to be quick to listen and slow to speak.

In Ephesians 4:15 Paul writes, "speaking the truth in love, we must grow up in every way into him who is the head, into Christ." The notion of speaking the truth in love highlights the relational context for our words. Truth telling does not refer to disembodied statements located "out there" bearing no relation to the community within which we stand. In fact, only when communities are infused with the love of God are they safe enough for real truthfulness. A truth-filled community holds together truth and grace, and speaking the truth in love requires gentleness, humility, and tenderhearted strength, despite our tendency to associate truthfulness with piercing insight and explosive criticism.

A commitment to living truthfully allows a community to be safe for the awkwardness of confession and for the long road to forgiveness and healing. Such communities depend on fidelity, the assurance that we will not abandon or misuse one another as our weak points are revealed and as we move in fits and starts toward holiness and maturity.

People who love the truth will use words carefully and use them to help rather than to harm. In a culture that is overfull with careless,

---

30. Hannah More (*Religion of the Heart* [New Orleans, LA: Paraclete, 1996], 129), quoted in Diane M. Komp, *Anatomy of a Lie* (Grand Rapids, MI: Zondervan, 1998), 122.

false, demeaning, and destructive words, the monastic emphasis on silence and on the avoidance of unhelpful or unnecessary words comes as a shock, something so countercultural it seems both impossible and very refreshing.

A love for the truth also means that we will resist impulses to "spin" situations in ways that are self-serving but not truthful. This is a temptation for Christians who want to have a "good" testimony. To avoid bringing dishonor to church or community, persons choose instead to stretch the truth or to omit aspects of the truth that are relevant but awkward or unbecoming.

Truth telling certainly includes an element of discernment or wisdom about what is fitting, which makes the practice more complex. Furthermore, there are cultural differences in how truth is spoken, and some patterns of truthfulness are more indirect than the "in-your-face" approach favored by most Americans. Nevertheless, whatever the style that is used, in every life-giving community people speak the truth to build up, not to tear down.

A community that loves the truth will have to fight human tendencies toward self-deception. People who want to be good but also want to do what they want are ready targets for this temptation. Stanley Hauerwas notes that we choose to stay ignorant of certain things we are doing; in fact, we fail to acquire the skills that would challenge our performance because we want to keep doing those things.[31] Thus, a truthful community will rehearse what it is doing, spelling it out.[32] The danger is that the more we want to be good, the more vulnerable we are to self-deception. If we do not care about integrity, we are not likely to feel a need to deceive ourselves or to hide something from ourselves by compartmentalizing aspects of our lives.

There are other reasons that we hesitate to be truthful and to live truthfully. Sometimes our reluctance results from a desire to protect ourselves or someone else. Power differences can make telling the

31. Stanley Hauerwas, *Truthfulness and Tragedy* (Notre Dame, IN: University of Notre Dame Press, 1977), 82.
32. Hauerwas writes that a self-deceived person or community "persistently avoids spelling out some feature of [its] engagement with the world." *Truthfulness and Tragedy*, 86.

truth much more costly for some than for others, and those with power can demand truthfulness but not offer it themselves.

Truthful communities will not necessarily be tidy. There will be loose threads and rough edges because such communities are unwilling to cover over wounds lightly, claiming peace when there is no peace. Truthful living involves forbearance, fidelity, patience, and engagement.[33]

Hospitality

As a community responds to the grace and truth it sees in Jesus and receives through Jesus, it turns outward in love and hospitality. A community that understands itself as having been invited into God's purposes and to God's table offers welcome to others as an expression of its gratitude.

Vibrant communities are dependent on strong relationships. And relationships are fostered through daily acts of hospitality, through shared meals, giving attention to one another, and taking time for conversation. Communities grow as they invite strangers into networks of life-giving relationships.

Offering consistent expressions of hospitality is not easy, but if the quality of our communal life is the best apologetic we can offer for the Gospel, then the practice of hospitality will necessarily be central. One of the communities I visited during my research on hospitality was Jubilee Partners, an offshoot of Koinonia Farms in rural Georgia. They welcome about thirty-five refugees every three months and help them adjust to a new life in the United States. The community of Christians that does this is very winsome; they have created a vibrant shared life with single people, families, and children. This small group of Christians provides small groups of refugees a chance to begin their lives again. It is an amazing community, as Christians and refugees from many different places make a life together, but it is on a very small

---

33. In the Psalms the word that was often formerly translated as "truth" is now frequently translated as "faithfulness" (*emeth*) and means stability, truth, trustworthiness, faithfulness, or verity. This shift demonstrates the close connections between understandings of truth and fidelity.

scale. What is most surprising in their story is that this community also welcomes three thousand visitors a year, mostly North Americans who have come to see the quality and beauty of their life together. So, at Jubilee Partners, we find a handful of Christians, thirty-five refugees, and hundreds of people looking on.

Most persons who live in community can recount similar experiences where their hospitality and community speak far more powerfully than their size or activities might suggest. Communities in which hospitality is a vibrant practice tap into a deep human longing, but also into the core of the Christian faith. Offering welcome to strangers is deeply countercultural because hospitality today has mostly been trivialized or commercialized—to many, it means coffee and donuts, dinner parties, or the hospitality industry.

To understand how and why offering hospitality to strangers is such a compelling practice, it helps to consider the biblical and historical tradition within which the practice was a central part of the identity and common life of the people of God. The biblical stories are rich. From early in the tradition, we read about Abraham and Sarah and the strangers/angels they welcome in Genesis 18; it is a story of hospitality filled with promise and blessing. At the end of the New Testament we encounter a picture of Jesus in Revelation, standing at the door and knocking, and promising to come in and eat with whoever opens the door.

Hospitality, welcome, and shared meals run through the biblical accounts. The gospels are filled with stories of Jesus as a guest in various people's homes, as a stranger who is sometimes welcomed but more often rejected, and as a host who feeds hungry crowds, makes room for prostitutes and little children, and cooks breakfast for discouraged and puzzled disciples.

God is pictured as a host in the wilderness, supplying manna every day, and later Jesus says that he is himself the manna, the Bread of Life. Jesus is not just a host or a guest, he is also the meal, the sustenance we need, the source of our lives. We read also of the extraordinary enactment of hospitality in the Eucharist. In that special meal, we remember the costly welcome we have received into the kingdom, and we are regularly fed at the table of the kingdom.

The earliest Christians understood the importance of hospitality. They knew that their welcome had come at a great cost, and that to be God's people, the members of God's household, the brothers and sisters of Jesus, they would need to embody the same character and to practice the same kind of costly hospitality. And so they welcomed one another into their homes when fleeing persecution or when traveling to share the Gospel. They ate together regularly so that the poor would be fed and so they could keep their new Christian identity alive in a hostile world. They worshiped in homes in the first centuries. And importantly, hospitality was the context within which they worked through very complex and troubling ethnic and status differences.

Based on the story Jesus tells in Matthew 25 about the final judgment, in which the separation of sheep and goats is tied to whether or not Jesus was welcomed and fed, and on Jesus' teaching on the kingdom in Luke 14:12-14, where he says to the host that the poor and broken should be invited to his parties, the ancient church was convinced that Christians had to open their doors to poor people and to strangers because it might be Jesus who was knocking (also Heb 13:2). In fact, hospitality was a central practice of the church for the first fifteen hundred years, and has stayed central in some monastic and intentional communities.

Like the other practices, hospitality is not exclusively a Christian practice, but it has distinctive features when embodied in the Christian community and shaped by Christian theology. Christian hospitality partakes of God's grace and reflects God's graciousness. Writers from the fourth and fifth centuries, working from the biblical texts, argued that hospitality should be generous and uncalculating, not offered to get something in return. Instead, it was especially to be offered to those who did not seem to have the ability to repay the kindness.[34]

34. This was in contrast to other understandings of hospitality that offered it to "worthy" recipients, those who would be able to give something in return. Hospitality always included family and friends, but for Christians it was meant to go further, to extend love and care and welcome to strangers, the least of these, the ones who could not return the favor. A special effort to welcome the poor, sick, disabled, and those the world overlooks characterized historic Christian understandings of hospitality.

Communities that practice hospitality today understand that the best gift they have to offer needy strangers is their friendship and fellowship. Far more than providing services to people in need, they welcome persons into a shared life in which they offer not only their resources and skills, but themselves. They provide settings in which strangers, guests, and friends can share their gifts because they understand that there is nothing more devastating than not having a place in which one's life and contributions are needed and valued.

Recovering the practice of hospitality challenges our cultural emphases on tasks, efficiency, and measurable results. Hospitality takes time, and opportunities for welcome can sometimes seem like interruptions. Potential hosts are concerned about risks, especially in welcoming unpredictable strangers. Homes are very private and often empty. One of the extraordinary blessings of community is that it reduces the risks and distributes the work of welcome over a number of people, such that hospitality is more readily sustained. In fact, throughout the tradition, the most significant expressions of hospitality to strangers were located in the overlap of household and church—in monastic and intentional communities and in home-based small groups.

Conclusion

Hospitality is a means of grace, but not only to those who are the recipients of welcome. It is a crucial way in which individuals and communities grow in virtue, Christ-likeness, and in dependence on God's strength. Welcoming strangers is a powerful corrective to a community's inclinations toward self-absorption. Communities that desire holiness and maturity continually hold in tension the nurturing of a communal life with opening it to strangers.

In the practice of hospitality, it is easy to see the close connections among the various practices. Communities that offer welcome to strangers also learn how important making and keeping promises are to sustaining relationships and common tasks. They discover the necessity of truthfulness and the dangers of deception and secrecy. They find that their lives are renewed by gratitude and forgiveness, worship and rest. These practices, learned in community, are also crucial to making community life both possible and good.

Summary of Audience Dialogue with Christine Pohl

When a participant observed that Christine had not included forgiveness among the four practices at the heart of community life, she responded that both forgiveness and discernment are really crucial but operate at a different level than the other four. They work when either practices collide or the deformations are active. The practices that developed happened in an inductive way, in the sense of looking at what was currently *not* being addressed in the literature. While a lot of material has been written on forgiveness in the last number of years and need not be rehearsed again, discernment needs a lot more attention.

The importance of discernment is enormous, especially where either sin or finiteness interacts with the practices, or where there has been some kind of betrayal. But we cannot necessarily address discernment straight on because of the impact it will have on other people's lives or the question of how you do truth telling in already broken communities. Learning to do it together by having the other practices in place at the same time, working toward strengthening the other practices, makes discernment more possible. The elements of trust and of time—both that we address the tensions at the right time but then we allow time to work through some of these problems—turns out to be very crucial.

A participant asked: In talking about the grumbling and negativity in community earlier, how does one discern the differences between justified criticism as part of truth telling and grumbling that is a huge poison? Christine responded: Being able to discern the difference between grumbling and truthfulness, that some of the community does not want to hear, has to do with how fidelity is operating in that context. If people know that the words come out of love and out of concern for the community, there is a difference. If the well-being of the community is absent, a self-centered approach that is all about me, it is not so hard to discern. There are other times where it is more subtle and less clear. Fidelity and hospitality operate in the larger context, in terms of receptiveness, openness, and being careful about how we hear things. Again, in all the practices one needs to be careful about how issues of power and authority operate. What are some good practices for the practice of gratitude that are neither a duty nor some kind of warm fuzzy? One can be intentional about setting aside times in which we are deliberately grateful for the people God has given us. Mary Jo Leddy's book *Radical Gratitude* has some very helpful suggestions in it: the Hebrew prayer *Dianu*; and some kind of liturgy: "If you had only taken us to the Red Sea and had not helped us cross it, we would still be praising you." There are complexities in getting people to be grateful and also a never-ending kind of attention to giving particular thanks, because somebody gets overlooked or some work is more invisible and yet very important. So, you have to be careful. There are ways of nurturing a common life that is attentive to the beauty around us, often coming from the leadership in fairly subtle but naturally embodied ways, rather than demanding it. Practices open up into life, whereas duties have a heavy, draining character to them.

Another participant shared that it seems that rules can become a replacement for gratitude and wondered about how to express gratitude via e-mail, when this medium seems so sterile and impersonal, even harsh or heartless at times. Christine observed that in the group of pastors who were conversing about truth telling, a number of them stated that they share nothing negative over e-mail, only affirmations and information. The more difficult, troublesome matters are handled face-to-face. More attention has to be given to the practices of grace in the context of e-mail communication. The relationship between gratitude and rules is an interesting one—the suggestion that when gratitude devolves into rules a community, after it has stopped the natural sort of gratitude, has to structure itself. It suggests the idea that gratitude can be on multiple levels: the gratitude toward God, the gratitude that is a sort of cultural environment in which we can be grateful to one another. The spontaneity of gratitude is sufficiently life-giving that a lot of things don't have to be put into clearly articulated rules initially, because people are more ready to do it. But in this culture, in which a certain steadiness of purpose has not been cultivated, a lot more things have to be articulated, not necessarily as rules, but at least as expectations.

An audience member offered the following example of expressing gratitude. Once at a monthly gathering of their intentional community, they were moved to share what they called "the desserts of their lives." The group is called "Bread of Life," so this wordplay was a celebrative thing that emerged out of an upwelling from the community. Talking about the desserts of their lives serves as "part of the leaven that lets the rest of what's happening rise." It is not unlike spiritual direction, where one practices noticing where the movement of God is afoot: the difficult things, countermovements, and backpedaling away that are brought to that place of grace.

Another noted that the discussion about the proper exercise of truthfulness would seem to require the exercise of gentleness and the practice of patience as fundamental. Moreover, patience has to do not with just cognition and volition but with affections and the exercise of emotions and so forth. Why is not patience one of the four grounding practices? Christine responded that her claim is not that these are THE four practices that ground community life, but rather they are ones that have been neglected. In the work with pastors, they cover quite a lot of issues, including patience. For her, patience probably fits into conversations about fidelity, as a sort of staying there and enduring. There are so many other things that could also be addressed.

An exchange occurred around the issue of hospitality: what is the relationship of growing up in a large family where neighbors and guests were always welcome and the practices of hospitality in the community? Christine responded that in discussions with her students about hospitality, the ones who have grown up in large families, oftentimes farm families, or are international students, can't imagine why they have to have this conversation at all, clearly because it is still a way of life in so many cultures. Hospitality in the household is really the primary location of the practice. Healthy families have enormous opportunities to do formation around the practice of just welcoming people into their home, but it is not as commonly practiced anymore because fewer people are home to welcome people into their shared life. The closing remark of the session connected gratitude with Eucharist, which is the great thanksgiving—the wider context of gratitude.

Newcomers to Monastic Life

Peter Funk, OSB; Vicki Ix, OSB; Peregrine Rinderknecht, OSB; and Beth Wegscheid, OSB

Peter Funk, OSB:[1]

Thank you to the Monastic Institute for the invitation. I am only a relative newcomer to monastic life—I've actually been in the monastery for almost eight years now. On the other hand, I am a real newcomer to a particular breed within religious life as a religious superior. As a dependent house of Christ in the Desert my being prior in our house means that I am the local superior.

Because I'm a native Chicagoan, when I became interested in monastic life I was quite surprised to find a monastery almost in my backyard. The monastery is only about three miles from where I was living at the time. It seemed providential to me that this was a community where I could go and pray and take retreats; I got to know the community and so entered in 1997.

Pinpointing what I value the most about monastic life is not very easy. I value the whole gamut of values within the life, especially its radical Christian commitment. But if I were pressed to choose one

---

1. Reverend Peter Funk, OSB, is the prior of the Monastery of the Holy Cross, a contemplative community in the Archdiocese of Chicago. Before entering monastic life, he was a choral conductor at the University of Chicago. He earned an MA in theology from Saint John's School of Theology•Seminary, Collegeville, Minnesota, in 2002, and was ordained to the priesthood in 2004. His liturgical compositions have been used by several choirs and communities in the Midwest and in Colorado.

or two elements, I would isolate Benedictinism's reliable spiritual discipline, which is based in a very balanced understanding of the human person and human community—something that is readily found in Christian antiquity but not so prevalent today, as Christine noted. But also, it has a spirituality rooted in the Scriptures, which I value very highly.

As far as what I find most life-giving in monasticism, certainly Scriptures and the sacraments continue to be very life-giving for me, but these I had "in the world." To look specifically at what is different about my life now, I would say this adjective "life-giving" gives two different but related meanings, experientially speaking. So, the common commitment of many brothers to the same goals often *energizes* me and makes me feel full of life, especially early in the morning when I'm lamenting having to sit through an hour's worth of psalms I don't care for. It's nice to have other brothers with me for this. Also, I am thankful for times of *lectio divina* to know that my brothers are with me doing this same practice, seeking God at the same time.

On the other hand, theologically speaking—and, again, I would agree with Christine that we are often handicapped in thinking in these categories—Jesus Christ is the Life. To answer this question fully I would need to ask, "How does Christ most effectively enter my life through my monastic life?" Abbot Notker spoke for me and for many seasoned monastics here when he suggested that Christ comes to us in distressing—or maybe a more politically correct term would be challenging—disguise in the oddities of my brothers. This doesn't feel life-giving at first, but we also know that when Jesus would expel demons from those who were held captive, at first people would say, "Oh, he must be dead," for they'd see the person convulsed. And so, the initial approach of the Lord is often accompanied by puzzlement or challenge or something that doesn't feel life-giving. But the commitment to stability, to the permanence of the vows, makes it possible to see in retrospect that actually Christ was active in this situation. What happens is this real, eternal life that we are given is one that disposes us to allow grace to expand our hearts to be able to love all kinds of people, and at all kinds of times to learn patience and humility.

And thus the particular challenges I've experienced come in this same way. I will enumerate them very briefly. The first is that it's just difficult to make a commitment these days. It's difficult when we don't experience community as life-giving in the first sense that I mentioned: when we are looking for joy and peace and happiness and what we find is our own desires and plans getting thwarted instead. The tendency for many young people today—and I include myself still in that group—is to recognize that sticking it out will bear the fruits and not giving up.

The second reality is that this project is undermined when there are these breakdowns in community: when there is not fidelity, when there is not truth telling, and this is a big obstacle because again in many ways our culture encourages and makes it easy for monks, even in solemn vows, not to be very truthful, and not to keep their commitments. This challenge affects every community today.

Finally, as a friend recently put it to me, listening accurately is a great challenge. It's easy to listen for information. It's difficult to listen with the kind of patience and attention that allows us to know really what's going on in the other person.

I want to conclude by saying that the whole range of prayer and work in the Benedictine life really gives a full context to these challenges and allows us to see them working toward our salvation.

Vicki Ix, OSB:[2]

First, I want to thank the planners of the Institute for their invitation. It's a very special honor to be part of the Institute this year as our brothers here celebrate one hundred fifty years of presence in Minnesota. I'm equally grateful for the opportunity to be in conversation with these new members of community and with our speaker, Christine Pohl.

---

2. Sister Vicki Ix, OSB, is a member of the Benedictine Sisters of Virginia. She received an MDiv from Saint John's School of Theology•Seminary, Collegeville, Minnesota, in 2002. Currently she serves her community as Director of Vocation Ministry.

I have been a member of the Benedictine Sisters of Virginia since 2002, and with the help of grace—or, as we say in Virginia, "Lord willing and the crick don't rise"—I hope to make perpetual monastic profession in 2007. I've been asked here to address what brought me to the life and to speak to the practices in our life that resonate in my heart as I continue to persevere. When I address the former question, I often think about how sneaky our GOD can be, is— sneaky in a good way. I think about how I found my way to the monastery by following a tiny trail of bread crumbs—what I like to call the "Hansel & Gretel School of discernment."

I came to this very place in 1999 to study at the School of Theology•Seminary. When I arrived in Collegeville—on a 100 percent Lilly Endowment Scholarship; thank you, Saint Lilly!—I had no intention of becoming a Benedictine sister. I had no idea what I would do with the degree, but I came here to get a degree that would open the doors to the varied ministries in our church for laypeople today— what Brendon Duffy likes to say, "Preparing to Serve" at Collegeville.[3] I began praying the Liturgy of the Hours with the monks and celebrating Sunday Eucharist with the sisters at Saint Ben's. It was in the company of these holy men and women that a truth about my life began to emerge and take shape. Morning Prayer and Evening Prayer with the monks felt right—"like holy bookends that [held] the day in some kind of sacred space."[4] The Eucharist celebrated within a monastic community of women was just a revelation. I was overwhelmed by the beauty of their liturgy and the warmth of their hospitality. Against this new horizon of monastic community I met a sister from Virginia who was on sabbatical at Saint John's. It would seem that I followed Cecilia Dwyer home because of her goodness and how she described her community. But I stayed because the community she described was real. I stayed because of the mystery of stability. I owe Saint Ben's and Saint John's a debt I can never repay.

---

3. Brendon Duffy is the Director of Admissions and Recruiting, School of Theology•Seminary, Saint John's University, Collegeville, Minnesota; one of the pamphlets on this school is entitled "Prepare to Serve."

4. Vicki Ix, OSB, "Testing the Waters of My Vocation," *VISION 2004 Guide*, 86.

Nourished and loved by both communities, I was able to make the next step and follow the bread crumbs all the way to Bristow, Virginia.

Having talked briefly about the Liturgy of the Hours in the context of my own discernment, I want to say something about how the Hours have come to mean so much more to me in the last few years. I've been blessed to study with Irene Nowell, OSB, here at the School of Theology and at the Monastic Institute and through the miracle of cyberspace in the virtual monastery. Everything I know about the power of words and the poetry of the Psalter I owe to her. Yet, I still can't quite grasp what we think we're really doing in those choir stalls. This part of our life is still very mysterious. We pray at a particular time and yet we pray outside of time. We echo the voices of the suffering and forsaken and, at the same time, we sing with the choirs of angels. If we are truly present to "the work of God," God is truly present to us in this mysterious enterprise.

At home we are a small house of thirty-five women and our oratory is really a circle of chairs that face each other. Just above the chairs on both sides of the oratory, there are three stained-glass windows made up of small, golden triangles. One evening as the sun set through the glass, I counted all the small pieces. Not my most prayerful moment. (Maybe you've been there.) But I couldn't help but smile as they added up to one hundred fifty. A coincidence, perhaps, but maybe someone wanted us to contemplate the gift of the psalms in our common life—the way they hold us together and free us to be one with the world all at the same time. Maybe someone understood better than I do that these one hundred fifty prayers are truly the jewels in the monastic crown. That they are, as Sister Irene says, "our daily bread."[5]

There are so many things about our monastic life that I cherish. But in the interest of time and brevity, I just want to talk about one more. I love how we do death. I do. At first, as a new, baby nun four years ago—and only in the community am I a baby anything. Out in the world it's called middle age. At first, Saint Benedict's admonition

5. Irene Nowell, OSB (personal communication).

to "day by day remind yourself that you are going to die" (RB 4.47) [6] seemed like a rather tall order. My own mother's death many years ago was almost more than I could bear at the time. I didn't know how I would survive loving these women that I live with and then, one by one, having to say good-bye. I didn't think I was the "strong kind" of monk that Benedict was looking for in community. Yet, as we've carried five women up the hill since I entered, the wisdom of his prescription has become clearer to me.

We promise stability—to live, to work, to love, and to die in one place. I love that we are to live each day as if that's all there is, with this God of the living who speaks loud and clear in the silence of the present moment. I love that, before death comes, we vigil with our sister—that we are never alone and are surrounded by prayer, loving touch, and even song. And when death comes, I love how we celebrate. The North American phobia of death, and efforts to avoid it, have no place in the house of God.

Our Vigil is a mixture of tears and laughter all held together by the Word of God. I'm already racking up some wonderful blunders that I'm certain will be told at my own wake one day. When the day of the funeral liturgy comes, most of us are usually ready to move from sadness to joy—ready to praise God for the gift our sister was and the glory to which she is going. By the time we lay her to rest, we have relived the paschal mystery in miniature—through one, small, beautiful Christ-light living among us. I really love how we do death. But maybe it's the way that we carry each other right now that really matters the most.

Peregrine Rinderknecht, OSB: [7]

As both the youngest and the newest member of this panel, and sitting in front of the abbot and community who will soon be

---

6. Timothy Fry, ed., *Rule of St. Benedict 1980* (Collegeville, MN: Liturgical Press, 1981), 183, 185.

7. Peregrine Rinderknecht, OSB, was born in Cleveland, Ohio, the son of a Lutheran pastor. His senior year of high school was spent as a student in Germany, where he met Lutheran Benedictine Sisters and became interested in monastic life. After

deciding whether or not I make vows in the fall, it is a somewhat ticklish thing to talk about the joys and challenges of community life. So, we'll start with how I got here, which is a little safer.

I met my first Benedictines in Germany. They were Lutheran Benedictine women—who were absolutely wonderful—at the Communität Casteller Ring that—strangely enough—started out as a Girl Scout troop and ended up as a monastery. It's a very long story. Anyway, on retreat there—a retreat around the psalms, I found both an attention to time and to community and also my fears about monastic life—that it would be cut off, cloistered in the bad sense from the rest of the world—were shown simply not to be true. These were truly loving women in the presence of God who loved and cared for all who came there.

Coming back to the United States, as the son of an Evangelical Lutheran pastor (albeit a very catholic Evangelical Lutheran pastor—I grew up in a parish with a tabernacle, and my father prays the Liturgy of the Hours and the rosary daily), I went to Valparaiso University in Indiana to study liturgy. I thought a long time about what it might mean to find a place of Lutheran monasticism in this country. There have been attempts. There is one Lutheran monk in Michigan who has striven valiantly for about forty years to implant monasticism on this continent in a Lutheran context and failed. He has lived a wonderful life but has had many people come and many people go. I wish him well, but that's not a struggle that I felt up to.

So, I sought elsewhere for community, heading out to Holden Village on the West Coast, which is an intentional community and intentionally transitional—no one is there for more than two or three or five years. About seven thousand people come through there yearly, which means that in the summer two hundred people can come and go on the same day. Falling slightly to the introverted side of the spectrum, I found that absolutely exhausting. At the end of

---

completing a major in liturgical studies at Valparaiso University in Indiana, he spent a year in community at Holden Village as the village potter and one of the cooks. Leaving Holden Village in 2003, he came to Saint John's School of Theology•Seminary, Collegeville, Minnesota, where he finished an MS in systematic theology before entering Saint John's Abbey.

the year I knew two things that I had discovered in this life: One, I needed to be someplace where academics were taken very seriously and practiced well; and two, that I needed to be someplace that was a little bit more stable. I didn't—at that point—think that I wanted to enter a monastery. I thought that I'd cleared that out of my system, everything was OK, and I was moving on to do my academic work, to teach somewhere. So, I came here and found myself sitting in a choir stall one Sunday and desperately feeling like this was something I needed to do. Of course, the first thought running through my head was "Oh no!"—an experience I've heard many other people articulate upon the making clear again that this is a life they might need to follow. But I have found this community to be a welcoming place with a broad view of the church that can welcome in all sorts of people and speak of what it means to live together under the Gospel.

So, then I entered the community in that fall as a novice. A lot of people say that the reasons that they came and the reasons they stayed are very different. I'm sure that's true on a certain level, but I don't think that I've been here long enough for it to be as true of me as it is for many of you. Many of the reasons for which I've come are still the reasons that I'm here. I'm sure the crises will come and that will work its way through. Over the last, almost ten years I've lived in one community or another (whether that's my undergraduate or Holden Village or the community here) that has prayed some form of the Liturgy of the Hours together daily, and I don't think that I could live without that. Yet, it's not a very easy thing to find. There aren't a whole lot of parishes that even have one piece of the Liturgy of the Hours in common, although there are some.

Secondly, stability has become a very major draw for me. As I mentioned, I was absolutely exhausted at the end of my year at Holden. Hospitality is important—hospitality is a piece, a major piece of our life together, but hospitality without stability, for *me*—I'm sure there are major extroverts out there for whom this would not be their experience, but for me—is impossible. I need to know to some extent with whom I'm going to be eating breakfast tomorrow morning. I need to be able to close the door of my room and not just have somebody walk in. Given that fact, I can then be more available to people. Putting lots of energy into commitments is much easier for me when I know that at least some of these people are likely to be here next week, next month, and the next decade.

One of the things I love about this life is that it is not subdivided. Growing up in the home of a pastor means that there's no such thing as a work/home division. People call all times of day. All of you in ministry know that it's very difficult to have a separated life—and I wouldn't want that now, truthfully. I can't imagine going to the office during the day and then coming home to a totally separate home life that didn't have anything to do with what I did the rest of the time. It would be hard for me to understand how those two pieces of life fit together and how each of them had meaning without the other one.

Finally, this place, like many communities, is one where the academic and the sacramental lives are held together. Both of those, I think, are deeply important to who we are called to be—that we not only talk and learn and listen, but we pray and receive the sacraments and come together to talk about how needy we are and to receive exactly what we need.

Of course, there are challenges for all of us. At our community retreat several weeks ago Sister Genevieve Glen said: "We might not like the taste of the heavenly banquet that is being offered to us currently, particularly in the Body of Christ with which we come to the altar, particularly in the community whom we know and who knows us." I think that sometimes the "being known" is the harder part of the Body of Christ to get used to, because truthfulness is something that—at least—I am still having to learn greatly. It's very hard, when living with this many perceptive people, to be anything but truthful, and it's very hard to be truthful.

The final challenge I'll say is that learning to live in community that crosses generations is, I think, a very difficult piece for our society in general today, but even more important is it true in our communities. The struggles, which many of my confreres have lived and to which they react, that happened in the '60s, the '70s, the '80s, and the '90s, are still very alive for them. A big piece of this year for me will be learning to take those struggles seriously, and while not living through *their* struggles, be aware of them and not be impatient for those struggles to just go away, as I need them to be patient with my struggles that are, again, different from theirs. It is just a question of patience and learning to live with each other.

Beth Wegscheid, OSB:[8]

Well, I can relate to that sense of humility, too. It's a little bit daunting to be addressing this topic and I am grateful for the invitation. I became acquainted with the Sisters of the Order of Saint Benedict in Saint Joseph since they staffed the grade school where I went, so I was taught by a couple of them—although sisters were on their way out of the schools at that time. But interestingly enough, my parents were taught by sisters from this community, as were my grandparents, which I didn't realize until I got here and I had a great-aunt who was also a member of this community. It wasn't until I was in college and had some of the sisters as professors and also as work supervisor in student development that I really began to know the sisters and began to detect something *very* different about these folk, aside from visible dress. There was a vitality, a sense of more aliveness and openness than I really was seeing in anybody else that I was coming into contact with—a joy that I found *very* attractive. I thought, I want that for myself! But the big question was, "Do I have to go to the convent to get it?" Well, ten years after college graduation, I decided, yah, I do. So, here I am. I've been here since September of 2003, and will come upon my one-year anniversary of first profession here next week.

8. Sister Beth Wegsheid, OSB, from Wadena, Minnesota, was a student of Bene-dictines who taught there. Her professional career includes psychology and human resources. She is a graduate of the College of Saint Benedict, Saint Joseph, Minnesota. She began discerning her call to religious life after becoming more acquainted with the sisters in college by participating in the Benedictine Friends Program. She entered Saint Benedict's Monastery, Saint Joseph, Minnesota, in September 2003. She made her first monastic profession on July 11, 2005. She has been a student at Saint John's School of Theology•Seminary and works on the Red Lake Indian Reservation, Red Lake, Minnesota.

So, what have I found to be most life-giving since entering? I'm going to borrow Father Columba Stewart's words and say it is the structure and being part of a spirituality that is substantial. That really is what I was searching for and what has been most life-giving for me. Part of it is being a part of something larger than myself, and part of that is being immersed in the Scriptures daily, all through the day, which I found to be *so* nourishing and life-giving, and to know that this story has gone on for thousands of years. It's not just here and now. It's not just fifty or a hundred and fifty years ago; it's something that started way back, with Abraham, and I'm part of it, too. And so, having that story illumine and give a sense of depth and meaning to my life has been very life-giving. When I first entered the monastery, I thought it was so odd, that sisters, first thing in the morning, would say, "Happy feast day!" And, "Happy this . . ." And, you know . . . when I turned thirty-three they said, "Oh, it's your Jesus-year!" And "Oh, it's your Die-year!" I said, "What is this?" I was just sort of shocked. I never heard these things before. Having lived that, I understand now how you *do* become immersed and that *is* your life, that *is* your story. So, celebrating the feast days, being daily immersed in where you are in the liturgical year, is just a wonderful thing, and it's not so odd anymore, although I don't think I've ever told anybody, "Happy Die-year!" So, it is just that sense of something deeper, wider, and broader. I really needed to be schooled in learning to pray in many, many other ways. Also, I really needed support. I couldn't do it by myself. I couldn't do it within the parish community—as wonderful as it was—that I belonged to. I needed something more, and I believe I've really found that.

Something else that I truly value about our community is the way that we celebrate—Sunday Eucharist, in particular, and feast days. We do that very well; we take the time and the care and the money that it takes—I mean—it's not simple to pull these celebrations together. That's not something I was particularly good at. And so, knowing that we do that is very, very life-giving for me; it has been a wonderful thing.

I have to say that being prayed for is one of the greatest gifts of being in community. Just about five minutes before this panel started, there were about seven of my sisters, who knew that I was nervous to come up here, and I know they've been praying for me. There's no doubt in my mind that I would not be where I am without having been held in that support and prayer, so that's something I appreciate. Also, we have shared silence together. Holy Week is amazing, for we hold silence. There's something so powerful about being in a place with people who are opening themselves to God and closing their mouths—still being attentive to each other, but allowing themselves and the rest of us, each other, to really expand and to meet God in a different way than we can when we're just busy and talking and going about our business.

There have been a few challenges. What is still a challenge, as I've moved from the novitiate into first profession and being more active and leaving campus to study and to work, is to be faithful to the monastic *horarium* . . . to make sure as I get busier that I still make the time for *lectio*. So, some of those personal disciplines I find challenging—but very much worth the effort and sticking in the struggle. I can echo Peregrine and say that intergenerational living has been a real challenge for me. While it has brought many blessings, it is definitely a challenge both ways, not just for me but for some of our elders, too. One of our elders told me, "I don't even *know* what the words you're saying mean anymore." That was a revelation to me and very helpful. I didn't realize that simply the way that I talked was a barrier to communication. Then one of the challenges that we newcomers have experienced is discerning that place of *how* much initiative to take, because I'm regularly told, "Oh, it's so good that you're here! You have so many gifts to share with us, et cetera, et cetera, et cetera. We want to hear your ideas!" Yet just knowing how much to initiate and how much to hold back and let things be as they are can be a challenge. I certainly don't have that one figured out, but I think I'm getting a little bit better at reading the cues. I'm just grateful to be here.

Dialogue of Newcomers to Monasteries with Christine Pohl

Christine: Thank you for this extraordinary description of life in community with points of truthfulness about some of the difficulties—so compelling and beautiful. I sensed so strongly that it was the good, faithful community and the people *in* the communities that actually draw people in. The apologetic significance and the compelling power of community ran through all your accounts. The community itself and the practices of the community together were so powerful to draw you into this life and make it possible to make the commitments. In a culture where it really is hard to make commitments and foreclose options, you really are countercultural. I was wondering what made it possible either in your formation or your experience even to imagine this kind of lifelong commitment that says, "I'm going stay; this is where I am; this is where I'm locating myself." Besides the winsomeness of the community, are there other things about formation and experience that would help us understand this?

Peregrine: I'll start with a little story. One of the things for me is the gradualness of the commitment. Investiture in the novitiate happens a couple of days before the Triumph of the Cross and then the year's previous class makes first profession on the Triumph of the Holy Cross in September. So, I was sitting there three days into the novitiate watching my friend Andrew make his first profession. The thought that came unbidden to my mind is, "Thank God, that isn't me." I didn't know what to do with that, and sat with it for quite a while, but I realized that for the first time in a long time, I wasn't looking forward to graduation and figuring out what I'd be doing next, or to the end of my year at Holden. Rather, I was required to be exactly where I was and not allowed to promise more than I was capable of at that point. I'm very grateful for that.

Peter: One of the factors that came up at the end of your talk is discernment. There is a very powerful tradition of discernment in Benedictine life, which means that the decision is not entirely in my hands. I can ask the community, "Do you think I should do this?" They say, "Yes!" And so I can take that confidently as something coming from God and not have to try to examine my feelings over and over again, which are so changeable. What gave me a lot of assistance is the reassurance of the community: if we didn't think you were suited for the life, we would be honest with you and tell you that you shouldn't stay.

Vicki: I'd like to echo that, too. I remember, long before I said anything to anybody about this insane idea that kept coming up in my head, I was having a conversation with Cecelia, who never brought up my joining the monastery. But one day, I asked her, "So, you know, what happens when a person wants to join your community?" She went over the flaming hoops you jump through and then she said something I didn't understand, "Before you move into the house we have a behavioral assessment." I said, "What's that about?" And she said, "Well, it's to find out if you have the skills to live in community; community isn't always good for everybody, and it's about your behaviors." I replied, "Well, so, you can *be* crazy as long as you don't *act* crazy." And she said, "Yah." In that little moment, I knew there was hope for me. I didn't say another word to her for four months! But that little glimmer of hope that you don't have to be some perfect, holy superwoman to become Sister So-and-So helped me because there's so much self-doubt in the process of discernment. As Peregrine said, the gentleness of God is so important. My life just got progressively downsized as I moved from professional life in the church to being a full-time grad student in a little tiny room in a dorm, so by the time we got to an eight feet by ten feet room at the monastery, it wasn't so hard. It was a very gentle process.

Beth: As we begin to study the tradition of the early monastics, there's so much richness there that speaks to our humanity. We are not called to be perfect, but we grow in perfection. We are called to be faithful. That whole sense of *conversatio*, turning, always turning, is a lifelong process. Hearing that spoken often has helped give me the courage to move forward.

Christine: I wonder if you could talk about truthfulness—the sense of your experience of expectations and the challenges of living in a community in which truthfulness is both crucial, but it is not so long since you've been in a larger community in which the same assumptions weren't always operative. Have there been times where you've been kind of taken aback at the transparency?

Vicki: Some of the sisters are absolutely without guile. Living out in the world for the better part of thirty-five years or so, I just wasn't used to that. What you see is what you get. That's a good thing, except when it comes to comments about the length of my hair. I always know where I stand with my sisters. And that's very refreshing. It took me the better part of two years, at least, before I stopped trying to be who I thought they wanted me to be—that was just getting positively exhausting. Everybody, maybe, hits that wall at some point where you just decide, "Oh, for goodness sake, I'm just going to be myself. You know, this is too hard. This is who I am. If this is going to work, God's going to make it work."

Peter: One of the surprises for me in that aspect is sort of the layeredness of truth—getting at the truth can take a long time. Sometimes I think I'm saying exactly what I mean and then I realize later, well, I left *this* out, or I left *that* out. The brothers have to be patient enough with me to try to articulate that again, to get closer to what I mean. Also, I have to allow my confreres that same luxury. Sometimes things are spoken in a context that doesn't favor a good reading of what they're saying. I just had an experience this past week where I'd assigned a brother to go on a certain trip and I knew that he didn't want to go. He hadn't said anything, but then some other things came up and he came to me and pointed out all these other things happening, and he'd be willing to stay home if I needed someone. My first reaction you could probably guess. So, I asked him about it and he said, "Oh, you know, honestly, I really didn't intend that at all. I just realized that the brothers, who were going to be left home, wouldn't have enough help and I didn't want you to think that I was going to try to get out of that work by this assignment." Finding the truth about the motivations of the brothers is very tricky. I come from more of an academic environment, in which we assume that the truth is univalent—one thing. But it's much more complicated than that. Living in community allows us to be OK with those unfinished ends that you were talking about, the pieces that don't quite tie up so neatly.

Peregrine: One of the really helpful things for me this year has been that our formation director expects us—in addition to *lectio* and private prayer—to spend about a half hour each day in *vipassana* meditation. That has been a time almost like, speaking metaphorically, when a brewer opens up a keg of beer; if he looks into the bottle, it looks totally clear and pure and you can see through it. But as soon as he takes that cap off, especially if it's an older bottle, it's gonna fizz and lots of things are gonna come out that he had no idea were there. For me that time has been a really important practice that I wouldn't have done on my own; the fizz comes out without even necessarily thinking, "Okay, now what was I doing here?" Halfway through, a thought will bubble up to the surface, "Oh, that's what I really did to that person today. I need to go apologize." It is just the space for a lot of things to happen that doesn't happen in a graduate school schedule, or if you're running around doing eight hundred things on your own.

Christine: Well, let's turn the conversation around now; since it's a both-way conversation, are there questions you would want to ask me in terms of some of the practices?

Peter: Could you comment a little more on the Eucharist, which came up at the end as something modeling thanksgiving for us? My experience is that because we come from an individualistic world, there is a tendency for men—even men who have been in religious life a while—to view the Eucharist in an individualistic way, as: "I'm receiving the Lord and my thanksgiving is simply a personal one," rather than being the case that we miss the opportunity for a very broad thanksgiving and gratitude in our life because we want certain things for ourselves out of the Eucharist; and not accepting again what the Lord offers us, which is the very human and also divine Body of Christ.

Christine: I think also that the Protestant traditions that have formed me have been extremely individualistic; that really is a challenge for us to more profoundly connect the Eucharist with community and its experience of one another. Attentiveness to the connection between Eucharist and gratitude and hospitality, as well as fidelity, in many ways, is a way of drawing out some of the connections of saying this is not just about me and Jesus, but this is about us. The individual element is a key part, but to have more of a sense of the *blessing* of being able to partake together and of *being* the Body together is only going to come with a combination of experience of doing it in community with attentiveness to some of the actual, physical arrangements and then some significant teaching on it in congregations.

Vicki: I'd love to hear more about gratitude. I thought when I came to the monastery that I was a person who had a grateful heart—until we had liver one night. I'm finding in my own tiny journey that gratitude has a similar challenge to hospitality in that it's always easy to be hospitable when you love someone, and it's always easy to be grateful when you're happy with what you've been given. But when the reverse is true, like when hospitality is *in*convenient or when there's liver on the table, how do we rewire ourselves to be grateful for *all* of it?

Christine: I don't know. Having lived long enough I know that one's a difficult question.

Peter: With regard to hospitality, we take turns being the porter each day, so we have a different brother on the door every day. We live in a very small space and one of the jokes that goes around is: the bell rings and if you see the person who's the porter, "*Deo Gratias!*" So, to a certain extent actually a sense of humor goes a long, long way in these things.

Christine: Absolutely! Absolutely!

Peter: Not to take what I have to get done quite so seriously, you know.

Peregrine: I have a similar story. I had a professor who liked to respond to that same kind of situation by talking about "Christ, it's you again!"

Christine: In a short presentation on any practice, we really can't get at the complexity. Gratitude is not a simple or just a happy practice. It's complicated by the fact that gifts come to us in broken people. There are gifts that we never ask for and didn't want, and gifts make connections between people that we don't necessarily want—and sometimes shouldn't have. Just like with hospitality,

there's a chronic tension in hospitality between welcome and boundaries. There is a certain naïveté to assume that we're not going to
encounter some kinds of real struggles that are tied to finiteness or
to sinfulness and so on. Sometimes it is part of a spiritual discipline
just to continue to nurture that gratitude in us. And sometimes it
really does require a certain amount of discernment and unpacking
to figure out the larger picture, not necessarily in terms of the liver,
but in terms of some of the more complicated things that undergird
some of the tensions in community.

Vicki: Then there are always the members of our houses—and
you can see them if you close your eyes—who never complain about
anything and who never say an unkind word to anybody. That gives
me hope. When you look around at all the holy ones who are forty
years down the track; the liver doesn't even phase 'em.

Beth: I think being newer also to the community, the idea of
offering hospitality can be really difficult. Because, for example, we've
divided our monastery into smaller living groups and so, if I would
want to invite somebody to one of our shared meals together within
the smaller group, which we do occasionally, it really is taking a risk.
Because I know that for some of those with whom I live it's more
difficult for them to offer hospitality because of introversion or because of health issues or whatever—they are a bit up in age. So, that
is a tension. One night, one of the sisters in my living group invited
somebody to our table, which was wonderful, and the thought had
never even *occurred* to me. I was a little alarmed by the fact that my
thinking had shifted. Also, there's that tension of being sensitive to
the needs of those with whom I live.

Christine: Right! Always there is the tension between members
and guests, and then the effect of some guests on other guests. It's
time now to open up the conversation to other people who would
like to be part of it, so we'll take questions.

A Pastor: I serve a Lutheran Church with one hundred twenty-
two members, and I often wish I had a bigger church, where the
pianist can play better than note by note. I had never really thanked
the pianist. I'm in my fifth year there, in this little church. One Sunday, as I was getting the elements ready for Communion during the

offering, I noticed that somebody was playing a really beautiful Mozart selection. I looked up from preparing the elements for Eucharist, and it was Nancy, this pianist who had always been chop, chop, chop, miss a note here, miss a note there. I just impetuously said, "Hold it! Who is that playing?" Nancy raises her hand. I said, "Thank you, Nancy!" in front of the sixty or seventy people that were there. Well, Nancy has also been a very antagonistic church council member—difficult to get issues through. Well, we had a council meeting right afterward that Sunday. She came up to me after the church council meeting and said, with tears in her eyes, "Pastor, thank you for having the church applaud for me for that piece." In five years of playing the piano whenever no one else would show up to play piano, she had never been thanked. It was a big lesson for me—that gratitude even in the context of a parish, against her fidelity, is so important. We can't keep the fidelity going if we don't have the gratitude.

Vicki: I think that's a wonderful story that also illustrates separating people from their issues. You mention that she was also very difficult in the council setting. Sometimes it's hard for us living in community with one another to keep the person—the child of God—separate from whatever the issues are that we're dealing with between each other. You're a wonderful example of that.

Peter: I think that raises one of the difficulties I've noticed: oftentimes the lowest maintenance and most competent people get thanked the least. It's very easy to ignore the people you really count on.

Beth: It just occurred to me when I was preparing for this panel, how much listening is a part of hospitality and how difficult it is to do, that is, how demanding it is to really listen. It strikes me that the first word of the Rule is "listen," and, as Christians but also as Benedictines and monastics, listening really is one of the practices that we are to cultivate. Hopefully we do through our listening to God in the Scriptures, in *lectio*, and at the Liturgy of the Hours and all that, but I feel really strongly that that needs to spill over into how we treat each other, too. It's demanding because oftentimes it doesn't happen conveniently; there are those who would corner us for unknown periods of time, if we allowed it. Sometimes we avoid them so we don't have to take it upon ourselves to listen for a while, and then disengage when we really must leave because that kind of assertiveness is very difficult, too. Listening is so much a part of allowing people the room to be who they are.

Observer: I come from a more pluralistic culture than what I see looking around the room here. One of the subtle problems we have sometimes with hospitality is that people in other cultures have a different understanding, which Christine alluded to earlier. I can just give one example of a religious community that was sitting down for dinner and the doorbell rang, and it was a student and his whole family, who were Hispanic, and the community was not. The community was very put out that they didn't call a couple hours ahead of time, so they could prepare enough food. The family wanted to be very nice, but they had no clue as to the nature of the coming at the time of the meal was OK, even if you didn't notify people ahead of time. So, as we move forward and have more diverse people in our communities, we're going to have to learn more about their own customs, cultures, and ethnic backgrounds as we embrace them with our hospitality. Hospitality is very culture-bound. We have to be able to open that more.

Christine: That's actually probably true of all the practices—that they have particular cultural settings in which they occur. But I am struck by the story about hospitality because there are differences in expectations; there is a difference in terms of hospitality as entertaining in the sense of having everything ready and making sure it's perfect before we have someone over. Then oftentimes in cultures where hospitality is very much more a way of life, people are welcomed to life as we live it. This latter way is really a much more helpful model, but it's going to take some work to recover. Also, when I was talking before about the experience of truthful speaking, one of my experiences with working at Asbury with international students is the difference between how we speak the truth to one another and the issues of indirectness. I'm learning that being indirect is not being untruthful; we really have to learn the ways in which a community understands how their being truthful and faithful. Fortunately for Christian communities, there's at least some shared commitments from which we can then work toward understanding some of the cultural differences.

Question: I was struck by the reflection on the practices that undergird your experience in community, that we all exist in varying degrees of community. What are the supports for or the challenges to your practices of community within your closest community from broader circles—family/friends, or oblates, or the broader ecclesial community? How can those who are connected to you in a larger circle be supportive or at times challenging to your practice of community?

Peter: Briefly, both aspects are connected to how well one knows the Benedictine charism and how much one is willing to trust that what the community is doing is actually right. I find that one of the ways to be supportive is just to trust that the community is doing what it's supposed to be doing by understanding that a lot of that is hidden work. An easy way to undermine the community or cause stress is to insist that it do something that it is not called to do. We get a certain amount of pressure being a monastery in a city. We have a lot of visitors who say, "Why don't you have a soup kitchen?" We don't want to say we simply don't have the time for that, but we really aren't called to that; it's really not our charism. We need to focus on our prayer.

Vicki: We have a rather large, extended community, not just for the Sunday Eucharist, but in our life in general. The ones who are dearest to me—mostly oblates—are the ones whom we have allowed to come into our life in such a way that they see us as fully human people, living together, trying to do the Gospel way, which means that they witness all kinds of craziness in our house, in our kitchen, and in our dish room, you know. They also see the constant practices of forgiveness that we have with each other. So, the shattering of the illusions that they might have about our life is a real gift to us because they don't expect us to be more than what we are, and they're willing to share our struggle.

Peregrine: One of the real joys of being here for the sesquicentennial has been being able to meet and hear about people whose families have been important pieces of this community's history. For example, Mike Roske works in our woodworking shop and we have a picture of his great-grandfather's family that was taken by one of the monks in the late 1800s. There's all sorts of people like that in Stearns County who are tied up for this house in its work with the university and its work with the parishes and all those other wonderful things that couldn't have happened without all the people related to the community who helped them. But I think the question is, then, how do you keep those centrifugal forces from just continually pulling out and out and out, and keeping the centripetal forces that hold everything together sort of stable in the center? I hope somebody knows how to answer that.

Beth: My experience of the other communities to which I belong has been that they are very supportive of my life in community. My family no longer expects me to be home for holidays. It's a question: "Can you come home?" Or: "This is what time we'll be having our holiday meal. We'd love to have you. Let us know if you can be there." The same is true with my friends that I had prior to coming. My experience of our oblates is that it's incredibly edifying to know that there are all these other folks around us who find this way of living life giving, valuable, worthwhile. When they come to pray with us, it's a wonderful thing. When they come to be with us on a Sunday for Eucharist, it's a wonderful thing. When they come and speak with us and share their story, it lights a fire, reanimates, and gives me a little bit more energy and a push to continue on this path because they are witnessing to me. So, thank you.

Section III

Monastic Women's Experience of Community Life

"Above all, the contemplative dimension is so central to living a Sabbath dimension, so we have time to touch the still center of our lives. In fact, this contemplative dimension holds together the different strands of our lives, integrates everything and makes our lives whole. There has to be a life of balance, a rhythm of creative leisure, of space for the sacred, a place where we can live and move and have our being in God. . . . Interiority, reflection, mysticism are what we all need, and what so many of us, in or out of monastic life, earnestly seek."

— *Margaret Malone, SGS*

How Women's Experience of Monastic Life Can Speak to Hungers for Community Today

Margaret Malone, SGS[1]

As I addressed myself to this topic, an amazing experience occurred in my own country of Australia, which set me thinking upon a particular line. Two men were trapped by a rockfall in a gold mine in a small town in Tasmania, one of the states of Australia. They were found to be alive after five days, housed in a cage about four-by-four feet. It took another nine days to rescue them in a very complex rescue operation. The amazing thing was the sense of hope that was exhibited by them, their rescuers, their own town community, and in fact by the whole country. People prayed and talked and waited, joined by one thing—concern for the two men and hope that they would be rescued. That sense of hope gripped me; I noted how a crisis such as this could stir up hope, even in the most desperate of

---

1. Sister Margaret Malone, SGS, a member of the Sisters of the Good Samaritan of the Benedictine Order, is a Benedictine scholar specializing in ecclesiology, history, liturgy, and spirituality. The title of her doctoral thesis, completed at the Australian National University, is *Things both Old and New: A Study of Authority in Benedict, Polding and Three Australian Benedictine Communities*. She has been a teacher in the Roman Renewal Program for English-speaking Benedictine women and a retreat director. Her Australian Benedictine Order celebrated its one hundred and fiftieth anniversary in 2007. She is a member of the *Communion Internationalis Benedictinarum*, the international association of Benedictine women, both nuns and sisters.

situations. I wondered if we members of women's monastic communities do in fact offer such hope to a world living in destitute times, a term of the Indian poet Tagore, and used by one Australian lecturer and author, David Tracey, in a recent lecture. Can we be women of hope?

A second point, by way of background, struck me forcibly as I thought about Saint Scholastica, who for many of us is considered to be at the heart of women's monastic life. There is a story in the *Dialogues*—the life of Saint Benedict—when Scholastica wanted to stay the night and continue the holy conversation with her brother at the end of her once-a-year visit. Benedict had stated that it was completely impossible for him to remain outside his cell for the night. She prayed, and such a storm ensued that they were unable to leave, and so, "they passed the whole night in vigil and each fully satisfied the other with holy talk on the spiritual life."[2]

The point to note refers to the writer's comment that follows. Benedict wanted the good weather to continue, but "contrary to his wishes and by the power of almighty God, he found a miracle coming from a woman's heart."[3] Then the text continues. "Nor is it any surprise that the woman who wished to see her brother for a longer time was on this occasion stronger than he, for according to the words of John, 'God is love' and by an altogether fair judgment, she was able to do more, because she loved more."[4] Longing for eternal life united the brother and sister—an insatiable desire, the text says. And the commentary on this story notes, "so in Gregory's story, love and power over the heart of God go together. One is the measure of the other."[5] The comparison between the degree of love of Benedict and of Scholastica is not the point here—the point is: what can be done by a woman's heart and by love.

2. Gregory the Great, *The Life of Saint Benedict*, Commentary by Adalbert de Vogüé, trans. Hilary Costello and Eoin de Bhaldraithe (Petersham, MA: St. Bede's Publications, 1993), chap. XIV.xxxiii.4, 155.

3. Ibid., chap. XIV.xxxiii.5, 155.

4. Ibid.

5. Adalbert de Vogüé, "Commentary," in Gregory the Great, *The Life of Saint Benedict*, 161.

So, to begin, women's monastic communities can offer hope and love to a world hungry for community. Let me set this perspective in context.

An Overall View?

To begin, let me tell you how I developed a perspective on women's monastic life. Over the years, I have had contact with many different monastic women's communities in Asia, Europe, the Pacific, and especially with communities in America and Australia. I learned that there are as many ways of living Benedictine life as there are communities. Each community has its own history, responds to particular needs of time and place, but lives a common way of life based on the Rule of Benedict (RB). Despite my limited perspective, I believe the points I raise will apply to women's monastic communities as a whole and probably for the most part to all communities. Living by the same Rule, the Rule of Benedict must surely bring about common emphases as we are all formed by the same values, even when our circumstances differ.

Communio Internationalis Benedictinarum (CIB)

Over recent years there have been strong developments among monastic communities of Benedictine women with much interaction and dialogue. They are now represented by, and belong to, a group called *Communio Internationalis Benedictinarum*, commonly called CIB. This group is indeed developing and emphasizing a global perspective on women's monastic life. By telling something of the history of this development, hopefully one will see the benefits of such a group and understand how I can, in some way, speak of what affects all women's communities.

Each monastery of Benedictines exists in its own right, though each may be loosely connected into some confederation. In the late nineteenth and early twentieth centuries, there were moves to establish structures for networking between congregations of Benedictine men in order to further the common tradition of Western monasticism. After the Vatican Council, when all communities were looking to their renewal and studying their sources, it became clearer that something similar should exist for women. A commission for nuns and sisters was set up and consisted of two separate groups—one for nuns and one for sisters. By canon law nuns are those who were enclosed and who take vows, recognized as solemn by the church. Sisters take what are called simple vows, which are less binding, and are not bound by enclosure.

Gradually, much progress was made in the way groups of Benedictine women met and shared things that were important in their lives. In 1972 some of the women were invited as observers to the Congress of Abbots. Then a much larger group met in Rome at the celebration of the fifteen hundred years since the birth of Benedict (1980), but the women were still only guests at a meeting of men. Gradually the nuns and sisters began to meet, and in 1988, under Abbot Primate Victor Dammertz, the two commissions of nuns and sisters merged, and delegates were appointed to represent eighteen regions throughout the world. It now has nineteen regions. It had become clear that a group for women Benedictines was needed to parallel the Congress of Abbots.

In November 2001, after a consultation process with all monasteries of women around the world, the CIB was formed and named. This was the culmination of a long struggle where in the first place the vision had to do with equal rights. However, the result has brought about something far deeper and wider.

The CIB meets at different places around the world and has met in Rome (2000), Nairobi (2001), Sydney (2003), Assisi (2004), and in Poland (2005). In 2002 a symposium on chapter 72 of the Rule of Benedict was held in Rome, and in 2006, also in Rome, there was a symposium on Wisdom Leadership. By meeting in different places like this, bonds and understanding of different cultures are created, the delegates learn about inculturation and globalization, and mutual understanding grows. The mutuality is attitudinal in the growing respect for different communities and practical through exchange and assistance. Many sisters from other countries and cultures have visited or stayed with communities in various regions, often for renewal or study. There has been a broadening and understanding of each community's vision of community as people share experiences. A pool of international experience is building up from which the way forward is becoming clearer.

In the development of the CIB, there is an emphasis on creating a friendly structure with possibilities that (1) enable Benedictine women across great differences to speak with a common voice, and (2) enable the giftedness of Benedictine women to contribute to the good of the whole.

The way the CIB operates also strongly models new processes and good collaboration. The leadership by the current moderator, Sister Máire Hickey from Dinklage, Germany, has been a very important factor in the development of the CIB. Benedictine women from all communities have growing understanding of other communities and issues of global significance for all. Benedictine women can see even more clearly than before the call to be aware of the world scene in order to make concerted decisions to help Christians live well in this world of ours, often a world of darkness. Communities have to be convinced that each one has a Gospel message for the world. As Sister Máire said in her report after the 2005 meeting in Poland, spirituality is something to be lived, but it needs to be formulated and communicated. Benedictine women must live, formulate, and communicate the Christian way of life through their existence and through their monastic hospitality. There cannot be a compulsive focusing only on one's own community.

Rather than speaking of monastic women's experience in particular countries, my emphasis will be on what is common to all the communities as seen through the lens of my experience in my own community. But because of what has happened with the CIB, and because of knowing so much more about each other's communities, it is possible to speak of the experience of Benedictine women in a general way through the particularity of my own community.

One Particular Community

Our community is called officially Sisters of the Good Samaritan of the Order of Saint Benedict (with initials SGS). We were founded in Australia in 1857 by an English Benedictine from Downside, John Bede Polding, who was the first bishop of Australia. In an era where Benedictine sisters were traditionally enclosed, he wanted what he called "a new Australian Benedictine institute," and he founded us so that we could minister wherever there was need, and in particular to women. Indeed, there was much need in this wild, early Australian colony founded on the lives of convicts shipped from England.

There was already at the time another Benedictine community of women in Australia that had come from England and lived very much as European Benedictine women of the time. Polding recognized the problems that could emerge about enclosure, which is why he wanted a new Australian Benedictine institute and set about establishing our community. American Benedictine women would relate to all this, as their beginnings were in the same historical period, though also different in many ways.

Polding described the scope and character of this new expression of Benedictine life in Australia in the nineteenth-century language of his time. "This congregation of Religious is designed for the practice of the spiritual and temporal works of charity, under the guidance of holy obedience, according to the Rule of St Benedict. Therefore . . . the Sisters are ready to teach in schools, to visit and assist the sick in their own homes and in hospitals, to instruct ignorant persons in the faith, to conduct Orphanages, to reform the lives of penitent women and to apply themselves to every other charitable work."[6]

So, Polding established a community of women whose lives were to be based on the Rule of Benedict and whose priority was to help women (and others) in whatever way there was need. Other monastic communities would not express it in quite the same way, but all would recognize these values and have hope, love, and compassion at the heart of their lives.

6. John Bede Polding, *Rules of Polding: an annotated translation of the 1867 Italian text*, ed. Pamela Pullen (Australia: Pax, 1982).

Our World

Is there any way monastic communities can share what is so important in our lives with a world hungry for community? This world of ours can be afflicted with such things as the need to be more competitive, more selfish, more individualistic, to work faster, to focus on the short term. According to Meg Wheatley, many people live in a world where there are no pauses, no paths, no pattern, no past, no future. People can suffer from poverty, oppressive leadership, tragedy, uncertainty, and yet human beings keep wanting to learn, to improve things, to care about each other. The human desires for freedom, meaning, love, are always emerging.[7] People are hungry for truth, a sense of purpose, and a chance to share their lives; they want to be generous, to be useful, and to experience peace and stability. We all look for gestures of love in our lives. We do not want dividedness, violence, injustice, but rather integrity, the "hidden wholeness" of things, transformation.[8]

Communities of Women

So, how can women's monastic communities be credible witnesses to, and share with, this world of ours, a way of life that is whole, that is marked by gestures of love? Parker Palmer defines community as a group of people with a shared commitment to making an external impact of some sort, from changing one another to changing the world. He notes that community means never losing the awareness that we are connected to each other. It is about being fully open to the reality of relationships, relationships that are neither invasive nor evasive, a community where deep speaks to deep, where we can learn to speak and to listen.[9] We cannot practice private

7. Margaret J. Wheatley, *Turning to One Another: Simple Conversations to Restore Hope in the Future* (San Francisco, CA: Berrett-Koehler Publishers, 2002), 7, 8, and 15.

8. Parker J. Palmer, *A Hidden Wholeness: A Journey Toward an Undivided Life: Welcoming the Soul and Weaving Community in a Wounded World* (San Francisco, CA: Jossey-Bass, 2004), 1.

9. Ibid., 54, 56, 113.

discipleship if we want to put the world in contact with the living power of the Gospel. We, as monastic women, want to do this in one way or another. Discipleship is not just commitment to Christ in the privacy of one's heart, though it begins there. It sets our agenda for Christian action.

Table and Oratory—Two Images of Community

Over a long period I have been interested in the teaching of Benedict on exclusion from the community in the Rule of Benedict, chapters 23–30. On the surface, these chapters are very off-putting, but there are treasures of wisdom hidden here. Two images, I believe, give shape to how monastic women live out their discipleship, and in doing so, model and share with others how hungers for community may be fulfilled. The two images are that of the table and the oratory. These two important areas of monastic women's lives are a sign for any group that tries to live out the values of community. In these chapters, Benedict imposes exclusion from the table and the oratory when faults are committed. By this obviously very serious punishment he must have seen the table and oratory as central to the cenobitic life.

When a less serious fault is committed, the monk is to be excluded from the table, that is, he is to eat after the community has eaten, and to take a lesser role in the common prayer. For more serious faults, he is excluded from the table *and* the oratory (RB 23 and 24). No one is to associate with him at work or meals or prayer, the purpose being that the monk has time to reflect on what he has done, to repent, and then ultimately be reintegrated into the community. This set of chapters in the Rule ends with the phrase *ut sanentur* (RB 30.3)[10]—that they may be healed, the purpose of the exclusion. But it is obvious that exclusion from the community is only significant and a cause of healing, if the monk in fact loves the community and feels strongly being separated from it.

---

10. Timothy Fry, ed., *Rule of St. Benedict 1980* (Collegeville, MN: Liturgical Press, 1981), 226. Hereafter all references to RB will be from this version.

Benedict and the Table

So, what does it mean to see the table as central to our community living? Many aspects of our lives stem from this—both in symbol and in reality. Let us see what Benedict has to say about the table as a central point of the cenobitic life. For him, the table is far more than the place of nourishment by food, though it is that, for Benedict gives specific chapters to food and drink, which show how important the meals are (RB 39, 40). But it is also a place of service, done in love—the brothers are to serve one another in love (RB 35.1, 6). The washing of the feet by the monks, who are to serve for the week and have served for the past week, is the great symbol of service in love, as it was at the Last Supper on Holy Thursday night when Jesus washed the feet of the disciples, before "he loved them to the end" in his passion, death, and resurrection (John 13:1; cf. RB 35.9).

The table is a place of presence and companionship where hospitality is expressed—the provisions for the kitchen for the guests are very specific. Two competent brothers are assigned to this kitchen, and they are to be given help when needed so they can do the work well and without complaining (RB 53.17, 18). The table is also connected to prayer, for the same verse of Psalm 70:2—"God come to my assistance, Lord make haste to help me"—is prayed by those who are to serve as well as opens the Divine Office in the oratory (RB 35.17; 18.1). The monks who are serving are to be given a drink and some bread, over and above the regular portion, so that they may serve without grumbling or hardship (RB 35.12-13). Two kinds of cooked food are to be provided, so that a person who may not be able to eat one kind of food may partake of the other (RB 39.1). The fact that Benedict gives all these details shows that he considers the table very important.

There is also spiritual nourishment to be given at the table (RB 38.1): "Reading will always accompany the meals of the brothers." The reader too begins with a prayer used at the Divine Office: "Lord, open my lips, and my mouth shall proclaim your praise" (RB 38.3; cf. 9.1); and, like the servers, is given a drink of diluted wine before he performs this service, no doubt so that he can perform the service well and without grumbling (RB 38.10).

Community and Table

From this teaching of Benedict some points about the table as a central symbol of any community will be expanded. Referring back to the story of Benedict and Scholastica mentioned earlier, the *Dialogues* state that after the whole day devoted to the praises of God and to holy conversation, as night fell they ate their meal together. During the meal Scholastica put her request to Benedict that they could talk on till morning about the joys of the heavenly life. After Benedict's unwillingness was overridden and they had to stay, "they passed the whole night in vigil and each fully satisfied the other with holy talk on the spiritual life."[11] Three days later Benedict saw the soul of his sister leaving her body and "penetrating the secret places of heaven under the form of a dove."[12] In fact, their conversation at the table had indeed been a conversation that penetrated the secret places of heaven.

I believe that in any community the table is a place where such conversations and hence such mutual support and encouragement of one another can happen. The quality of our relating at the table is a sign of how we share in the eucharistic table; an expression that we are living in communion. Hopefully it can never be said that we live in community, but not in communion, for our living in communion is meant to draw us into the mystery of the Trinity. Deep sharing can happen at the table (a literal one or a symbolic one) when people are in communion with one another. At the table our search for meaning and for God and being raised onto another dimension of things that are beyond the here and now can be realized. Truth can be spoken, hope engendered, friendships deepened. New ways of imagining our world can arise through our sharing, and we can be impelled into action.

A story is told in Australia of Sir Ronald Wilson, the man who was appointed to lead a commission set up to investigate the appalling treatment that had been meted out to our Aboriginal people. In speaking about his experience he said, "I sat, I listened, I was moved and grieved by what I heard and I was changed; and now I cannot

11. Gregory the Great, *The Life of Saint Benedict*, chap. XIV.xxxiii.4, 155.
12. Ibid., chap. XIV.xxxiv.1, 155.

do other than live out my new convictions."[13] Listening and conversation can move us and change us. One of our government leaders speaking at an Aboriginal conference said, "If we can only learn to talk quietly with one another, honestly with one another, openly with one another . . . we will arrive." It is indeed all *together* that we go to everlasting life (RB 72.12), as Benedict says, and we must grow together through relating and sharing deeply. We need to be experts in humanity, in our acceptance of one another, as well as being experts in theology.

Another thing our sharing at the table does is to confirm us in our identity. We feel a sense of belonging; we can discover who we really are and be at home. There can be real mutuality here. Benedict often expressed this idea with the word *invicem*—"one another." The cardinal-archbishop of Westminster, speaking to the monks of Downside Abbey in England in March 2006, noted that monasticism teaches us the art of belonging to one another.[14] There is a giving and receiving, an appreciation of a variety of gifts, and a reverence for others. Benedict reminds us in the words of Paul, "each has a particular gift from God, one having one kind and another a different kind" (1 Cor 7:7; RB 40.1). This reverence and acceptance of others are the outcomes for those who, according to Benedict, hold nothing dearer than Christ, who set the love of Christ before everything else. One of the main ways that we find Christ is in one another, and our sharing at the various tables of our lives can help this to happen.

Christ in One Another

There is another beautiful story from the *Dialogues* in the context of the meal, and in particular a paschal meal. A priest, who had prepared a meal for the Easter festivities, saw the Lord in a vision,

---

13. Sir Ronald Wilson remembered remarks at the launch of the document "Bringing Them Home: Report of the National Inquiry into the Separation of Aboriginal and Torres Strait Islander Children from Their Families." This document is available at the Reconciliation and Social Justice Library, http://www.austlii.edu.au/au/special/rsjproject/rsjlibrary/hreoc/stolen/index.html.

14. Cormac Cardinal Murphy-O'Connor, "UK Cardinal Praises Monastic Life," March 19, 2006. See http://www.Cardinalrating.com/Cardinal_65.htm.

who said, "You are preparing delicacies for yourself, and my servant in such and such a place is suffering from hunger." So, the priest went searching for the man of God (Benedict) on mountains, in ravines, and in caves. He found him hidden in his grotto. Together they prayed, blessed God, sat down together, and after some pleasant conversation about life, the priest said, "Get up. Let us take some food. For today is Easter." Benedict replied, "I know that it is Easter because I have the honor of seeing you."[15] What a wonderful phrase this is, and how significant, if we could say it to one another in all truth. The story goes on to say that Benedict in his solitude had overlooked that that day was the solemnity of Easter. The priest insisted, "Seriously, today is the Resurrection of the Lord, Easter day. Cease your abstaining. It is not fitting on this feast. That is why I have been sent to you, so that we may eat together the good things of the All-powerful Lord."[16] They blessed God and had their meal. When they had finished talking, the priest returned to his church, nourished by the conversation as well as by the meal.

This section of the *Dialogues* continues with the story of the shepherds who found Benedict in the cave, were changed through meeting him, and began to visit him. "They brought food to sustain his body, and from what he said to them they took back in their hearts nourishment for life."[17] So, in the meal at table we recognize Christ in one another and take in our hearts nourishment for life.

Service in Love

The table is the setting for the washing of the feet, our service of one another, as chapter 35 of the Rule of Benedict teaches. For Jesus this was the ultimate service. After he had washed the feet of the disciples, he commanded them, "So if I, your Lord and Teacher, have washed your feet, you also ought to wash one another's feet" (John 13:14). Love makes us able to do this. Basil asks the question when

15. Gregory the Great, *The Life of Saint Benedict*, chap. II.i.6-7, 10-11.
16. Ibid., chap. II.i.7, 11.
17. Ibid., chap. II.i.8, 11.

speaking of the advantages of living in community over living alone, "Whose feet then will you wash? Whom will you care for?"[18] A beautiful Jewish saying states: "I learned the Torah from all the limbs of my teacher." We learn to serve and live the Gospel from such actions of Jesus as this.

It takes time, energy, and commitment to stay at the table, much like Benedict's workshop, where we must learn to live the Gospel by using the necessary tools over a lifetime. There is a beautiful story in a book by an Australian writer—Robert Dessaix.[19] He has just been diagnosed with AIDS, and when he comes home and tells his partner, Peter, Peter says, "I'll stay beside you all the way." We also have to stay beside one another all the way.

Authority

Moreover, our mutual sharing at the table can be a sign of how authority is to be exercised in a healthy community. Trust and mutual responsibility are part of this; so too the appreciation of the gifts of others. Benedict may not be speaking literally of the table when he calls the brothers to counsel, but the giving and taking of counsel before a decision is made by those in authority includes mutual sharing. There has to be a belief that each has a gift to offer, and that the good of the whole is the responsibility of each one. A listening with the ear of the heart (RB Prol. 1), as Benedict says, is a necessary quality in all, both those who lead the community and all the members. A good decision requires real presence and real participation at the "table" where discernment is happening, and the realization that this can take a long time with much sharing and back and forth.

Ultimately in Benedictine life, after long listening and consideration of all that has been said at the "table," the abbot decides. This

18. *A Life Pleasing to God: The Spirituality of the Rules of St Basil*, ed. Augustine Holmes (London: Darton, Longman and Todd, 2000), 142.

19. Robert Dessaix and Igor Miazmov, *Night Letters: A Journey through Switzerland and Italy* (USA: Picador, 1999), 11.

may sound very autocratic unless one understands all that happens in chapter 3 of the Rule, where the abbot has really listened to the voice of the Spirit speaking through all the members of the community and hence has carried out true consultation. There is nothing wrong with someone in authority making the final decision after such deep listening. In the end, good decisions come out of careful discernment by discerning hearts. We have to create spaces of quiet and freedom and dialogue. The diversity of gifts can then be directed toward a corporate mission, the building up of the whole body. This sharing has to be part of the "table" of our lives.

Table—A Sacrament

Finally, the symbol of the table and what it can teach us about living in community is that the table can reflect the sacramental and incarnational in our lives. The table is a sign of our unity and a reflection of beauty in our lives. Communities try to ensure that there is beauty at every table—and our experience can lead us to value more and more every aspect of beauty—music, art, literature.

The bread and wine shared at our ordinary tables are a sacrament of the bread and wine shared at the eucharistic table. The table is a sort of sacred site that reflects how we should live in this world with reverence for all creation. It is interesting that the root of the word "ecology" is *oikos*—house or a dwelling place. There is an Irish traditional saying that says, "It is in the shelter of each other that people live." As we live relationally in the shelter of each other, our attitude to the earth, our environment, and one another, takes on a sort of sacredness. Our sharing with those who have less or nothing must stem from this attitude.

Divisions at the Table

However, one thing that cannot be ignored at the table are the divisions, disruptions, and complete separations, which can happen at normal meals and at the table of our lives in our communities. The truth is that because of our human condition we do sin and fail—often. We are not always able to bring a perfect faith dimension to bear on our daily living. It is easy to paint an unrealistic ideal of community and to pretend that the struggles and difficulties should not happen. Nevertheless, hurt and pain happen often—yes, even for those who try to live in community.

Reconciliation and Forgiveness

What has to be done then? We have to learn how to make efforts at forgiveness and reconciliation. Otherwise our lives can be a sham. We have to learn to be honest with each other, to forgive not once but seventy times seven if necessary (Matt 18:22). Benedict advises making peace before the sun sets (RB 4.73), a good practice whenever possible. However, forgiveness and reconciliation after deep hurts can sometimes take much longer, so communities need to establish rituals that will help the members in this process.

Benedict suggests a very gradual process when the monk who has been excluded is to be taken back. He is gradually reintegrated into the community, first lying at the feet of all as they leave the oratory but still outside. Next he comes in and prostrates himself at the feet of the abbot and of all. Then he comes back into a place in the oratory but perhaps not his original place, and even then he cannot lead a psalm or reading until the process is completed (RB 44). Benedict, in his wisdom, knew that forgiveness and reconciliation—the making whole again—can take time and rituals can help. But there is no doubt in his mind that healing, forgiveness, and reconciliation *must* happen. Nor is there any doubt in the mind of anyone who tries to live in community.

The Oratory

The second important symbol of community—absolutely essential, and without which there would be no meaning or point to our lives—is the oratory. Prayer and faith have to be at the heart of our lives. All of us who live in monastic communities came to find our particular way of seeking God. This is Benedict's criterion for entrance into the community (RB 58.7). He asks, "Is there anybody here who yearns for life?" (RB Prol. 14). Monastic women seek life and God within the community. Others live out their seeking of God and their desire for fulfillment in different ways.

Above all, the contemplative dimension is so central to living a Sabbath dimension, so we have time to touch the still center of our lives. In fact, this contemplative dimension holds together the different strands of our lives, integrates everything, and makes our lives whole. There has to be a life of balance, a rhythm of creative leisure, of space for the sacred, a place where we can live and move and have our being in God.

People often say that Benedict does not have a lot of teaching on prayer. In fact chapters 8–20 of the Rule are mostly short and are centered around details for the celebration of the Divine Office. But he is really speaking about a life of prayerfulness where day in and day out we expose ourselves to the word of God through *lectio divina*—our reading of Scripture—or through the Hours of the Divine Office that make our days sacred. For Benedict, one of the criteria for those who are to enter the community is eagerness for the Work of God, that is, the Divine Office (RB 58.7). Through the word of God we are gradually transformed into Christ. Our life in Christ, begun at baptism, gradually reaches its fulfillment so that we can say with Paul, our life is *in* Christ.

Interiority, reflection, mysticism are what we all need, and what so many of us, in or out of monastic life, earnestly seek. Monastic women have committed themselves to a life where this is paramount. In the secret places of our hearts we have to listen for the transforming word that God speaks to us. Benedict uses the idea of heart often in the Rule: our prayer should be characterized by purity of heart or freedom from sin; compunction of heart, a piercing knowledge of our sinfulness combined with an awareness of what we could be; and humility of heart, or knowing our place before God. Finally, Benedict mentions *intentio cordis* (RB 52.4)—that powerful longing and yearning of the heart for God. The feast of the Ascension sums up all our longings for the beyond, for something more, for God. Augustine says in the text in the Divine Office for that day: "Today our Lord Jesus Christ ascended into heaven: let our hearts ascend with him."[20] Benedict says that we must yearn for everlasting life with holy desire (RB 4.46). This is what the contemplative dimension of our lives helps us to do.

Another text of Augustine speaks of the two aspects of life, one represented by Peter, who receives the keys of the kingdom of heaven with the power to bind and loose, and the other by John, who rested on Christ's breast: "for the sake of a most restful harbour of that life most withdrawn [from the world] the Evangelist John rested on the breast of Christ"[21] (Augustine, Homily 12 on Saint John's Gospel). It is a mistake to think that the contemplative dimension of life is not for everyone. Not only John, but all of us must draw from the well of the Lord's breast. In a Carthusian community in Italy there is a symbol over the door—two doves—representing the contemplative and active aspects of life, drinking from one fountain. All must have both aspects in their lives, though emphasis may be given to one or another at times or in different places. The wonder of communities of monastic women is that some may seem to live more in the world, some more separate from it, but all must in some way experience and integrate both dimensions of life. It is necessary to create an environment that brings the heart of each person into contact with the word of God and to let God's work of conversion take place. Our real journey in life is interior, that is, a matter of growth, of deepening, and of an ever greater surrender to the creative action of love and grace in our hearts.

The Question

The question in the title of this paper asked, "How can the experience of monastic women speak to the hunger for community

20. Augustine, "Sermon 263A," in *The Works of Saint Augustine: A Translation for the 21ˢᵗ Century*, Part III–Sermons, vol. 6: Sermons 230-272B on the Liturgical Seasons, trans. Edmund Hill, ed. John E. Rotelle (New Rochelle, NY: New York City Press, 1993), 222.

21. Augustine, "Tractate 124," *St. Augustine—Tractates on the Gospel of John 112–124*, The Fathers of the Church 92, trans. John W. Rettig (Washington, DC: Catholic University of America Press, 1995), 93.

today?" The experience of monastic women, as far as it can be generalized, can show to the world the possibility of living the values of community through behavior. Paraphrasing Saint Augustine on the call to authentic living, we can say: "Sing with your life. Make sure your life sings the same tune as your mouth."[22]

After Vatican II, one of the main emphases was to develop further a theology of *communio*. There was the call to identify, structure, live, and celebrate the experience of the church as a communion of disciples. Religious communities, by living as a communion of disciples, have to satisfy people's hungers for community on a human, religious, and Christian dimension. Communion involves relationships on a broad spectrum of practices: forgiveness, tolerance, forbearance, support, rejoicing, receptivity, faith. Communion is at the heart of our call to live the Gospel, how we do justice, so as to call the world to do justice, and how we model hope and assurance that it is possible to live justly.

I believe that all monastic women, whether more enclosed or not, will affect others because of the way we live, have been formed and transformed. Some may do this through various ministries in close contact with people. Some, remaining in the monastery, will do this through their interactions with guests or with those who work there or share in the prayer life of the community. One sister in an enclosed European community who takes care of the entrance to the monastery said, "I like that, to open the door without already knowing who is knocking and asking." Whoever is knocking and asking must feel extraordinarily welcome by such a person. This is the hospitality that the porter in chapter 66 of the Rule is to show: "As soon as anyone knocks or a poor man calls out, he replies, 'Thanks be to God' or 'your blessing, please'"; then he is to provide "a prompt answer with the

---

22. Augustine actually writes the following: "Listen to me—or rather, listen to God through me: Sing to the Lord a new song (Ps 149:1). 'Well I am singing,' you say. Yes, you are singing, of course, you're singing, I can hear you. But don't let your life give evidence against your tongue. Sing with your voices, sing also with your hearts; sing with your mouths, sing also with your conduct." See Augustine, "Sermon 34," *The Works of Saint Augustine: A Translation for the 21st Century*, Part III–Sermons, vol. 11: Sermons 20–50, trans. Edmund Hill, ed. John E. Rotelle (Brooklyn, NY: New City Press, 1990), 168.

warmth of love" (RB 66.3, 4). This is surely the model for all our in-teractions—whether we minister, within or outside the monastery, we must help all to make contact with the living power of the Gospel as Good News.

How do we draw our neighbor to God? Rowan Williams in *Silence and Honey Cakes* quotes Antony the Great, who says, "Our life and our death is to win our neighbour."[23] He then goes on to say that winning our neighbor means not judging him or her. If we do judge, we show forth a judgmental and unattractive God. If we do not judge we show forth a loving God. But the point shows that our life is always intimately bound up with our neighbor. The lives of all in turn are bound to the life of Christ and are a reflection of God. By our very being, how we live in community, and what we do, we can win people to reflect on their own lives and thence to be drawn to God. Even our weaknesses and failures can draw people to God because knowing our own sinfulness makes us less ready to judge or force or intimidate others. We will never do any of this unless we ourselves are first at-tuned to where God is leading us, unless we are first "won."

Hope and Love

I began this presentation speaking of hope and love. The main way to speak to the hunger of the world for community is to be mo-nastic communities of hope and love. Hope and love enable us always to see more, take risks, make sacrifices, and explore the unexplored. They also help us to cope with pain, loss, and struggle. Our lives, honestly embraced and authentically lived, are a source and witness of hope and love to all with whom we come in contact. Hope and love grow and manifest themselves through the ordinariness of our lives, and then this ordinary stuff of daily living opens the door to transcendence.

Very likely we do not know where we are being led. Dag Ham-marskjöld once said, "Never let success hide its emptiness from you,

23. Rowan Williams, *Silence and Honey Cakes: The Wisdom of the Desert* (Oxford: Lion Hudson Plc, 2004), 23.

achievement is nothingness, toil its desolation. And so, keep alive the incentive to push on further, that pain in the soul which drives us beyond ourselves. Whither? That I don't know. That I don't ask to know."[24]

The Australian writer Michael Whelan describes a life of hope in this way: "Hope filled people know in their bones that their story is part of a bigger human story. Their story in fact is part of a cosmic story, that is, in turn, part of an eternal story. There is our reason for hope, there is no other."[25] Our experience of living in monastic women's communities can show this hope a hungry world and can proclaim that there is something more to life than individualism, consumerism, selfishness, and despair. Even in this era where aging and smaller numbers at times make us wonder about the future, we can still have hope.

Recently I came across Roger Housden's book, *Seven Sins for a Life Worth Living*.[26] Perhaps the best way to summarize how the experience of monastic women could help assuage the hungers for community is for our communities to commit these sins. Housden then speaks of the pleasure that comes from each sin, and I paraphrase him here.

(1) The Pleasure of all Five Senses, because then we will treasure and savour all of God's creation, and live fully the implications of the incarnation and our sacramental sense. (Sensuality)

(2) The Pleasure of Being Foolish, because then we will relax and enjoy our lives, and not be caught up in competitiveness to be always successful and always on top. (Foolishness)

(3) The Pleasure of Not Knowing, because then there will be always something to learn, and we will be good disciples who

24. Dag Hammarskjöld, *Markings*, trans. Lief Sjöberg and W. H. Auden (New York: Knopf, 1964), 55.
25. Michael Whelan, "The Human Ground of Hope: A Pastoral Reflection," *Australasian Catholic Record* 82, no. 4 (2005): 463.
26. Roger Housden, *Seven Sins for a Life Worth Living* (New York: Harmony Books/Random House, 2005).

can be taught. Then we will have what Jean Leclercq calls the *Love of Learning and the Desire for God.*[27] (Ignorance)

(4) The Pleasure of Not Being Perfect, because then we will always know ourselves in our full humanity, and we will learn humility. (Imperfection)

(5) The Pleasure of Doing Nothing Useful, because then we can know true sabbath and real leisure and will have the right atmosphere for prayer. (Uselessness)

(6) The Pleasure of Being Ordinary, because then we can be content with who we are and be peaceful about accepting it. (Ordinariness)

(7) The Pleasure of Coming Home, because then it must be that we are happy, know we are in the right place, know acceptance no matter what, know we can return, and know we belong. (Prodigality)

Perhaps if we as monastic communities lived like this, it is enough, and it will speak to hungers for community today.

27. Jean Leclercq, *The Love of Learning and the Desire for God: A Study of Monastic Culture*, trans. Catharine Misrahi (New York: Fordham University Press, 1961).

Intergenerations in Community

—Part I

Teresa Jackson, OSB[1]

Over the last several months, Kathryn and I have had a wonderful opportunity to get to know each other through the miracle of e-mail. We've spent some time trying to figure out what on earth an intergenerational conversation would look like. Fortunately we came up with four central questions for discussion, which we took to "peer groups," if you will, gathering input from them on what their thoughts were on these questions. Those four questions are: (1) "What is the hunger you have for community today?" (2) "What helps and what hinders you in realizing that hunger?" (3) "What is most life-giving about and what hinders intergenerational living in your community?" and (4) "What are the most important issues for life together now and in the future?"

So, I'm going to share essentially reflections—my own and those of the newer people in my community, and then Kathryn will talk about it from the perspective of folks who have been in community longer.

1. Sister Teresa Jackson, OSB, is a member of the Monastery of Saint Gertrude in Cottonwood, Idaho. She made final profession in 2003. Originally from California, Sister Teresa has worked with the retreat ministry at the monastery and has conducted numerous retreats and workshops around the country. Currently she is the codirector of oblates and director of volunteers at her monastery. She has an MA in spirituality from Santa Clara University.

What is the hunger you have for community today?

The hunger that people have for community today is probably as deep as it is often hard to articulate. What most of us "new" people have in common is a sense of something lacking in our lives prior to coming to monastic life. For many of us it wasn't clear what that "something" was, but there seems to be a hunger that is both satisfied and challenged by community life.

Of course, everybody's story is different, but I suspect that my story is probably as unique as it is typical. When I came to the community, I was already forty years old and never married. Never raised in any church, I became a Baptist in college. Then in 1992 I joined the Catholic Church, which is a whole separate story that involves God's deeply strange sense of humor—a theme throughout my life, actually. As soon as I decided to join the church, which is quite an amazing thing right there, pretty soon I found myself thinking about religious life. Clearly this was not something I *wanted* to be thinking about. To put it very mildly, this was not a call I wanted to hear or respond to. So, I had a lot of very intense, not particularly happy, conversations with God about this along the lines of "Isn't it enough I'm becoming Catholic? Do I have to become a nun too!?" Well, God has God's own ideas.

Many people say they felt "led" to religious life. I always say that God dragged me, kicking and screaming. So, when I describe my "hunger" for community, I think it was a hunger for something that I knew was good, but I wasn't entirely sure I wanted.

Typical of many people entering monastic life today, I already had a fair amount of life experience: a good job, which I considered ministry, in the mental health field; good friends; and an interesting parish. But there continued to be this vague, nagging feeling that somehow my life, my relationship with God, was a little too shallow, wasn't really fulfilling. So, my personal call to monastic life was really that this life was simply, at its heart, nothing more or less than what all Christians are called to live: to seek God deliberately together in community, but, really, at a greater depth and with a greater intentionality than may be possible outside of religious life or other forms of community life.

So, for "my generation" this hunger for community is clearly very strong, as shown in the fact that to come to religious life today in middle age means giving up everything we've known. We have given up career or job, family—for many people that includes children, house, income, status, sense of identity, accomplishments; all those things just have to be chucked out the window to come and enter religious life. So, entering is a profound stripping of very fundamental aspects of oneself and one's identity. Now all of this is true whether you come at eighteen or fifty-eight, but the older you are, the harder it is because we've accumulated more not only material but also psychic possessions.

So, the hunger of this new, younger generation for community is deep, pervasive, and substantial. Even when it cannot be articulated or even experienced on a conscious level, it nonetheless impels people into monastic life today.

What helps in realizing this hunger and what hinders?

What helps and hinders, as most of us who've lived in community know, are really two sides of one coin: the reality of living day after day in the deeply satisfying, deeply messy midst of community. Living community, in all its incarnated glory and goop, is precisely what's most wonderful and most aggravating about monastic life. It's wonderful to be around women who have lived this life for fifty, sixty, seventy years, and who clearly have been molded and transformed by it. Of course, it's also rather depressing to be around women who have lived this life for fifty, sixty, seventy years and may not be models of what we hope we'll become.

Before I came to community I read a book by a journalist who spent some time with men's Trappist communities; he interviewed a variety of monks and abbots. At one point he quoted an abbot who said that living in community means "we all walk around naked here"—meaning that there's nothing hidden or secret in community.[2]

2. Frank Bianco, *Voices of Silence: Lives of the Trappists Today* (New York: Anchor, 1992), 156.

The Trappists are not alone in that reality. In fact, after a few months in my community, I really wanted to amend that statement and say, "we walk around naked in a house full of mirrors." It's not always an edifying sight!

So, to live in community means not being able to hide our faults, shortcomings, peccadilloes, or major neuroses. They just hang out there for everyone to see. On the flip side it is possible to experience being loved, accepted, and even on our worst days at least tolerated by the rest of community, despite our flaws. Life in community is life at its most absolute, stripped down, basic, where we have a choice as to what we'll make of that basic, essential life. Living in community, then, can mean being transformed, really beginning to bring about the reign of God in the midst of the world; or it can mean refusing to acknowledge and learn from our brokenness, from what we see in the mirror every day in our brothers and sisters. We just have to keep choosing every day. What's it going to be? Are we going to allow community to transform us? Or, are we going to refuse to look in the mirror and work on what we see?

Perhaps what helps most to create community is simply to admit that we are naked—out there, hangin' out—that we are flawed people doing the best we can with what little we have. So, what we need simply is to cut some slack for ourselves and for the other people with whom we live. In turn, community is most hindered when we refuse to admit our own brokenness, or we project it on other people, or we see it in the mirror and don't recognize it as ourselves, or we refuse to grant other people the acceptance and the love each of us needs so badly.

What is most life-giving about intergenerational living? And what hinders that intergenerational living?

There are a number of concrete issues that come from living with a wide range of ages and life experiences. The obvious advantage for us "younger" people, who haven't been in community very long, is we find ourselves in the middle of incredible wisdom from the *senpectae*, the women who have lived this life for so many years and pass their wisdom along to us. Here the image of community is like water on a rock, in which each of us comes with her own personal "rockiness" that is subjected to the "water" of community, day after day. So, many folks are then molded and shaped by the years of the water of community, to become monuments of humility and patience—just the translucence of really reflecting the light of Christ.

Others of us, on the other hand, are probably more like hunks of granite out in the desert who only experience occasional, seasonal downpours of this water. In other words, progress is really quite slow for us. But the lesson of intergenerational living is that it is possible to see what it is like to be molded by community, to have the edges stripped away, chipped away day after day, year after year, because of the grace of so great a cloud of witnesses surrounding us.

Yet there is another reality of intergenerational living: the fact that we really don't simply come from different generations, we come from different cultures. There's a huge cultural divide. In most of our communities the majority of sisters are those who entered before Vatican II. They know what it's like to wear the habit, to be sent out at eighteen with no training to teach fifty fourth-graders, and to manage to survive a whole summer on ten cents spending money. Such stories are, frankly, beyond most folks' ability to imagine. So, we're really living in the midst of an ongoing experiment in cross-cultural communication.

Another difference for most people in my generation is that we didn't come with the same images or the same experience of women religious. We're more likely to have had little substantial contact with sisters because a number of us are converts. Since most of us have been formed after Vatican II, we don't know the previous, pre-Vatican II Catholic culture that many people experienced. We don't know and really can't imagine the incredible struggles and changes of the '60s and '70s—that wasn't part of our experience.

Also, we often have different experiences of what it means to be in service/ministry to the church because our relationship to the church is substantially different, that is, we have not come to monastic community for ministry in the church.

Thus the most difficult part of intergenerational living is not the superficial things that are often focused on: not enough people to play volleyball anymore or to play pinochle (they let me make profession even though I refused to learn), but a much more subtle and maybe occasionally obvious clash of cultures and experience. Unless we are aware of and open to being in communication across those different cultures, then it is harder for us to grow, live together, and be formed in community life.

What are some important issues for life together now and in the future?

The usual issues that are mentioned are leadership, vocations, money—the practicalities of the future. But beyond these there is a singular, deeper, simpler issue for our life together in the future, which is, to paraphrase Benedict, "Do we have the good zeal necessary to bring us all together to everlasting life?" (cf. RB 72.2).

Good zeal isn't easy, for it means taking risks and loving people we don't like, even to the point of bearing their burdens. Good zeal means imagining new ways of being community because community, being together, relying on one another, is the way in which we come to salvation. Good zeal means knowing that we are loved by God, loved by our sisters, so that in turn we can show that love to the most broken in our community, to the most broken in ourselves. I firmly believe that it is precisely this good zeal that constitutes the indescribable force that has kept Benedictines around for over fifteen hundred years, through all kinds of crises and all kinds of transformations and changes. It is this good zeal that in turn will bring us altogether into everlasting life (RB 72.12) in this new millennium.

—Part II
Kathryn Casper, OSB[3]

As Teresa indicated, the only way that I can speak is also out of my own personal experience—that of a female monastery of practically a hundred and fifty years. Hopefully that experience will lead to pondering your own experience. I want to say a bit more about the cross-cultural that Teresa alluded to.

The title of this conference, "One Heart, One Soul: Many Communities," is surely inspiring, especially since this segment on intergenerational living reflects exactly the significance of that title. Within each of the several communities represented here are perhaps numerous smaller "communities," because we all bring our own particular worldview and our own particular circumstances to the community. Many of the intergenerational studies recently done in the United States refer to age cohorts, which describe the various worldviews that happened to people based on the time in which they lived. There is a coming of age that one experiences in a particular time in history. The particular worldview of a coming of age cohort in no way can describe the totality of any human person, but it does give us some indications of what might be some of the cross-cultural effects experienced in intergenerational living. So, for example, when I entered the community, the community had the dubious honor of

3. Sister Kathryn Casper, OSB, is a member of Saint Benedict's Monastery, Saint Joseph, Minnesota. She's been a professed member of the community for fifty-six years, during which she has been involved in a variety of ministries. She has been a teacher and principal, a designer and director of programs for separated and divorced, remarried, and widowed persons in the Saint Cloud Diocese. She was the director of women in first profession for ten years, while at the same time serving as a spiritual director and a presenter of programs. She has facilitated the discernment process of election of the prioress in a number of monasteries. Presently, as a member of the Spiritual Ministries Team here at the monastery at the Spirituality Center, she serves as a spiritual director; coordinates and co-teaches the internship and spiritual direction program; is a presenter at the Center, parishes, and other groups; and is the codesigner and director of our latest program called the Sophia Program for laywomen in ecclesial ministry. Sister Kathryn has her MA from Seattle University.

being the largest Benedictine community of women in the world. Imagine the complexity of all the different worldviews. Right now we have 304, so this is a very complex issue.

Let us recall the descriptions of these cohorts. In my own community very many sisters, who are eighty years of age and older, came of age between 1912 and 1921. The name of that cohort was the Depression cohort, not that they are depressed. They came of age during the time of the Depression; they are described as having an attitude of "waste not, want not" toward life. The World War II cohort, those who came of age between 1922 and 1927, is noted as seeming to have an ability to sacrifice for the common good. My own cohort, and if there is anybody here who has been in the community about fifty-four years or so, called the post–WWII group, is said to have conformity, conservatism, and traditional family values as hallmarks. The succeeding cohort—the familiar baby boomers, who make up the largest segment of the aging population in the United States, came of age during the turbulent sixties. So, we can imagine the worldview of those folks. Generation X appears to have the characteristics of a search for emotional security and independence. Generation Y, or "N," as it is sometimes called, faces the gifts and burdens of the technological age, and, while having every access to communication, may experience a lack of intimacy. So, our college students are born with a cell phone in their hand, iPods, e-mail, and everything else, but searching desperately for intimacy. Of course, there will be subsequent studies on all the other new generations. Moreover, each of these aforementioned age cohorts is marked by particular spiritual movements that add another layer of the variety and cross-cultural aspect.

In addition, as Teresa talked about, the most significant event in the Roman Catholic era of our time was the Vatican Council II. The enormous repercussions of that event that took place in the early 1960s are still either being celebrated or mourned by Catholics, depending on one's particular point of view. Let me describe my own entrance into community as part of that pre-Vatican segment.

Unlike most newcomers, I entered at age eighteen with no job or ministry to leave behind. Then it was taken for granted that one would be a teacher, or perhaps an organist or piano teacher, or work in our hospital, perhaps be a housekeeper in one of the local convents, or do some administrative work at the monastery. It was also understood by most of my generation that we would not live at the monastery. Now it is interesting to note that the place where we worked was called "the mission," and we were sent in obedience "out on mission." The monastery itself seemed to be a place for retired sisters, for administration and service positions, and for teaching in the college. This may seem a bit strange to newcomers, who have left job and service because of wanting to live the monastic life at the monastery.

What is worth considering is that because most of my generation served in some church-related ministry, we perhaps had a different picture of the place of monastic life in the life of the church. Teresa alluded to that. It seemed that we had an understanding of the importance of the church's mission in the world. Moreover, monastic life has always played this role, even though Benedict does not speak specifically about that in the Rule. Surely the fact that we called our places of living away from the monastery "missions" is quite revealing.

Then came Vatican II. The events marked by that council happened forty years ago, and so, of course, newcomers to the monastery have no lived experience of the enormous changes and adaptations that were made by my generation. We feel that we have earned some of the changes that have been made, which for the most part many of us are happy with, although some desired never to make the change, or have never been able to accommodate themselves to the changes in dress, customs, and lifestyle.

Therefore, even within my own age group, there are "many communities." Last night I talked about all this with the sisters in my living group. One sister remarked, "It's amazing we can all live together as well as we do." We talked about how this can be so, and recognized some of the reasons why we are able to live intergenerational life, which are enumerated here:

- We are each committed to one way of life and one love, while it may have various expressions.

- For the most part, we have come to accept and integrate those various expressions.

- Certainly the common celebration of the Eucharist and Liturgy of Hours constantly calls us beyond our individual selves to the larger Gospel vision of God's dream for the world. Certainly silence and solitude are very blessed things in a large community with a variety of persons.

- Over the years most women's monastic communities have spent an enormous amount of time and effort in learning new ways of communication and deepening our understanding of the monastic way of life, which is essential for community.

- And last, but first, the fidelity of God and God's continuing gifts of grace to us make it possible.

There are some challenges for newcomers to community at this time in history, too. As Teresa said, the very scale of the transition women and men entering the community are facing in today's culture is large. Some have left behind a home or apartment of their own, a car, other material goods, friendships, their own schedule of life, and being able to make most decisions based on their own interests. Most of the newcomers had very responsible jobs and were used to using their gifts in successful and creative ways. Many had a rich and deep spiritual life before coming to the community. So, perhaps for someone entering a community it can seem that none of this is truly recognized or is not important. Sometimes members of communities forget or do not acknowledge that these women and men had a life before they entered community—a poignant reality, especially for women who enter and have been married with children.

I worry a little about the newcomers who will be the future community because those entering may be few in number and may not have as many things in common among themselves across the stages of formation as my generation did. With twenty of us in the novitiate, I was surrounded by women who came from my own cohort. We all lived the pre-Vatican way of life, which was regimented, with clear expectations. So, differences did not seem as enormous as they do now. While the newcomers may form friendships and collaboration with other sisters in the community, sometimes I wonder what intentional efforts are made to assist them in forging bonds of respect and collaboration among themselves. These efforts cannot be left to chance because the newcomers will be the new community, the future community. There needs to be an intentional undertaking to assist these women to forge those bonds. It is the responsibility of both the newcomers in formation and the recently professed to find processes that encourage the development of a community of respect among themselves, bridging the differences that they might find among them.

Since some women/men who enter Roman Catholic monasteries may have been only recently received into the Catholic Church, or had little experience living as a Catholic Christian, they perhaps need time to integrate both the Catholic *and* monastic way of life. There may be a need for more undergraduate or graduate theology and practice. Certainly I would like to see newcomers take advantage of theology and monastic study programs here at Saint John's or elsewhere. I believe the future of our monasteries depends on a solid education and formation in Scripture, liturgy, monastic studies, and monastic spirituality.

Needless to say, this short list does not begin to name the challenges of multicultural issues of race, religion, or lifestyles. Finally, the face of the monastery, the church, and the world will continue to change dramatically. Will we be ready for this newness? Will those of us who are older in community let go and let the newcomers, oblates, and associates take their rightful place in continuing the ancient tradition, but with unforeseen applications? I hope so!

In conclusion, there is a poem that seems apropos to our topic today: "The Sage Must Travel Light," adapted from the *Tao Te Ching* by William Martin.[4]

May each of us, newcomers and hopeful sages, carry only compassion for one another from one day to the next.

---

4. William Martin, *The Sage's Tao Te Ching: The Ancient Advice for the Second Half of Life* (New York: Marlowe & Company, 2000).

Dialogue with Teresa and Kathryn

Could these new sisters coming to monasteries be a kind of missionaries to oblates, just like the older generation of sisters were missionaries for the church?

Teresa: That's a wonderful image and insight. I certainly feel that the reality of the future of monastic life will be in forms and with types of commitments that we have not necessarily seen in the past. I am continually impressed, edified, and grateful for the commitment of oblates, folks who feel that this Benedictine way of life is so life-giving. I would hope that those of us who are newer in traditional monastic life can be some kind of bridge for new forms, new ways of being monastic in the future. Now, today, is a wonderful, exciting time of transition for monasticism.

Kathryn: In addition, just as the amazing rise of women in ecclesial ministry in the Catholic Church is not just a stopgap because women can't be priests or because of the shortage of priests, it is, rather, a real movement within the church. Your insight is right on, indicating the same thing about our times right now.

Are there any examples of processes to bridge the gaps among the younger newcomers?

Kathryn: One of the things that has happened among Benedictine women's communities is the Novice Institute and the Benedictine Spirituality Workshop and Retreat for women in first profession. These programs gather women from all over the United States and beyond to come together and meet each other, so that a woman who is alone in her monastery meets a number of women across monasteries. That is wonderful. What is also needed are processes within a monastery, certainly as large as ours, where the variety of women who are newly or recently professed or in formation could come together and begin to discuss together their lives, hopes, and dreams, perhaps to bridge differences that are between them or to form a bond.

Teresa: What ends up being the most important is not so much the formal kind of programs, although those are crucial, as when both the newcomers and those who have been in community longer are much more intentional about doing the hard work of bridging some of those cultures. Often people may be peers in age, but because their life experiences are so different, they end up not having anything clearly in common and so have to stretch more than perhaps otherwise, in order to find something in common. Often it is quite frankly easier to relate to folks older than I am and who entered later because we come from similar worlds. It is certainly worth the effort to get to know folks who come from a totally different world, and yet are amazing people.

Kathryn: In my community, when a woman who enters at forty-five or fifty, her peers have made their profession quite a long time ago and have formed bonds within the community. So, for that woman to break into the peer age group is not always very easy. These questions are very valuable.

Section IV

Community Life Now and into the Future

When Cardinal Joseph Ratzinger took the name of Pope Benedict XVI after the patron of Europe, Benedict of Nursia, to be the model of his papacy, Sister Joan Chittister, in a weekly column for the *National Catholic Reporter*, offered four major concepts from the Rule of Benedict as ways to proceed in his papacy. Those "four dimensions of Benedictine spirituality" are listening, humility, community, and hospitality.[1] The presenters and panelists for this section had been asked to reflect on these four dimensions in light of their own experience in community life.

1. Joan Chittister, "And He Shall Be Called," *National Catholic Reporter Online* (April 20, 2005); http://www.nationalcatholicreporter.org/update/conclave/jc042005 .htm.

Four Concepts of a Benedictine Community in the Twenty-first Century

Listening, Community, Humility, and Hospitality

Meg Funk, OSB[2]

Introduction

The design of this essay is to articulate "what is a Benedictine community?" from the classic point of view of what's intended by the Rule, then to see how the many communities can articulate what is essential for them. An idea came to me when I was in England recently from the wheelbarrow. They are in every garden. Just go under a tree; they are ubiquitous. The wheelbarrow, which I will call Ben, is really doing the work and points to what is really important.

2. Mary Margaret Funk, OSB, is a member of Our Lady of Grace Monastery in Beech Grove, Indiana. After serving two terms as prioress, from 1985 to 1993, Meg became executive director of the Monastic Interreligious Dialogue (MID) in 1994 and served in that position until 2005. During her time with MID she coordinated the Gethsemani Encounter in 1996, and Benedict's Dharma Conference. She has been widely engaged in interreligious monastic dialogue in India, Tibet, China, and all around the world. Today she serves as the director of the School of *Lectio Divina* at the Benedictine Inn in Beech Grove. She has published four books; she has a trilogy: *Thoughts Matter* (1998), *Tools Matter* (2001), and *Humility Matters* (2005) (New York: Continuum International Publishing Group).

My intention in this essay is to articulate the elemental, in other words, to abstract "what is it that we do when we do monastic community?" I will address the four concepts of community, hospitality, listening, and humility. Community is like the bucket of the wheelbarrow. Benedictines are cenobitic; they are a *koinonia* community in a cenobitic setting. Two shafts keep the community balanced and move it in one direction or the other: one is interiority represented by listening and silence; and the other is hospitality, the outward orientation. But it is poised, guided, parked, moved, and shifted altogether on the wheel of humility, placed firmly on the ground.

Part One: Community

What is a monastic community? What is in the bucket? What is it carrying around? It is a specific type of community. What distinguishes a monastic community from a utopian village or a utopian ideology, for one reason or another, is Christ Jesus. We were called, set apart, lifted up, to return to our original image and likeness as creatures created by almighty God through Christ. In this calling, this vocation, we repent, we change, we turn, and not just our heads, but our whole body, our whole soul, our whole mind. In this turning, we continue this *conversatio* and we do it together as a *koinonia*. *Koinonia* is a lived experience of community where, because Christ Jesus was incarnated in our midst as one like us, we become a *we*. We come together back to God through Christ Jesus as a *we*. The oxygen that moves between individuals is the *we*. *We* in the *koinonia* is not just any community; *koinonia* is explicitly mystical. The mission of the monastery is the monastery: the monastic way of life. In that monastic way of life we go as we go. Sometimes we are sent out in obedience.

Let us go back into Ben, into the container, and describe this calling, this vocation, this repentance. Then, what is our right effort? What is our experience of being called? What are we doing when we do it, when we come to the monastery and we live the monastery? To answer that question: we are awake, but we need to stay awake. We need to be conscious because Christ Jesus is living and active *now* in our midst, not sometime later. When we say our *suscipe*, our vows:[3] "Uphold me according to your promise, that I may live, and let me not be put to shame in my hope" (Ps 119:116), the expectation is to experience, to realize, to have a consciousness of Christ Jesus right now, right here, with these people, in this heart, in this body, in this plot of earth, in this container. It is not an intellectual concept; it is not in one's time off or in one's next lifetime; it is right here, right now. How do we sustain this consciousness? How do we sustain this actuality? How do we sustain living in this presence?

We sustain it by living in the elemental. Elemental means absolute purity of what we do, because the doing of it is both expressive of and constitutive of who we are.[4] We bow to one another because the Christ is in each one. We welcome the guest. We do the Hours of liturgy. We do the common meals. Margaret had a wonderful description of this in her presentation: in the common table, both in the nourishment of bread in Eucharist and the bread at our dinner tables, as well as in our conversation and presence with one another.

In fifteen years of East-West dialogue, I have learned immensely from my Buddhist and Hindu brothers and sisters. They have an "awakeness" about them that is very attractive. I can remember Dr. Norbu, the Dalai Lama's eldest brother, coming to Beech Grove

---

3. Vow language has been shifted for American Benedictine monastics to return to a literal interpretation of the Rule of Benedict. In this writing I am deliberately using the word "vow" for emphasis that this commitment through community is "to God" rather than a juridical incorporation into the group identity. While this flattened out language is an effort to be precise, nevertheless this usage diminishes the mystical sense.

4. Sister Jean-Marie Howe, OCSO, *Secret of the Heart: Spiritual Being*, Monastic Wisdom Series 2 (Kalamazoo, MI: Cistercian Publications, 2005), 50. In chapter 6 of her book, Sister Jean-Marie presents the **elemental**. As I understand it, "elemental" means "reduced to the essential." It is a rudimentary state, a condition that accentuates the fundamental components or principles of a given reality. The "elemental" refers to the origins, the ground, and the constitutive qualities of something. One might say that the elemental is like a space, an atmosphere, or a quality of being that yields itself to the essential, where everything is subordinated to and oriented toward the emergence of what is essential. The elemental, thus understood, becomes a "carrier" or an epiphany of the essential. All this suggests that an elemental condition or state favors the emergence and the experience of the essential. The essential, in its turn, designates the primary, the vital, the indispensable, and the necessary. The essential is the irreducible truth of a reality. The essential is our authentic identity and raison d'être.

Monastery and to Vespers; he was stunned. He said, "You know the word in Tibet for a Christian is 'one with no inner light.'" He found at our house, and he would find it here, great light, great energy.

So, for a moment, what would people find if our wheelbarrow people came to us and would enter into our community? This energy should be tangible, experiential, visible, palpable. It is as it is. It is much like attending a concert, where we feel something there. Our experience together should and does have an actual vibratory, calibrated Christ-consciousness. Let us see what is underneath that.

Christ-consciousness is something, not nothing. We experience it; we know it. So, when we go to the Liturgy of the Hours, morning, noon, and evening, and say: "O God, come to my assistance; O Lord, make haste to help me," that brings up our original repentance, our original turning toward God, our original "Sustain me, O Lord; accept me, O Lord," to calibrate to this vibration: "Yes, bring me back to it." Of this experience one might say, "Well, isn't that arrogant to say that I will always have an experience of God's presence?" If we do not have the actual experience of presence, we have the actual experience of faith. Our faith is that sturdy muscle that is brought to every prayer, to every meal, to every table of conversation, and to every opening of a workday. Thereby our Christ-consciousness is real. A monastery is a form to keep this Christ-consciousness alive, vibrating and conscious, awake and personal, actual, realized by each one of us and all of us together. So, the elemental is mystery; the elemental is presence; the elemental is really an experience of Christ in our midst. He said, "I'll give you the Holy Spirit" (cf. Luke 11:13; John 14:16). The Holy Spirit is nothing other than this undifferentiated presence that we experience. Furthermore, when we experience this presence of Christ Jesus in our midst, in our hearts, and in our actual flesh, Christ Jesus is redeeming in us (we have remained at table), but faith tells us and we experience it—Christ Jesus is working through us to continue the reign of God that he started when he became incarnate in our midst. So, you and I, when people see us and we see them, are there; it is Christ present through us.

During Gethsemani II, the exchange between Buddhist and Christian monks, we did rituals. In some rituals, the Buddhists participated just by observing the Mass and the Office; sometimes we watched their chanting, just respectfully being in their presence. A couple of other rituals we did together. The Buddhists did a teaching and an initiation of us into "loving kindness" *metta* practice, which was very profound. We tried to think, "What would be our ritual into which we could incorporate them? What would be appropriate?" William Skudlarek, OSB, had the idea, "Let's do the washing of the feet, like Holy Thursday." So, we did. Out of sensitivity, I washed the women's feet; William washed the men's feet. There we were together, with a white apron on and a towel—talk about elemental. The monks behind us in a little *schola cantorum* were singing *Ubi caritas*. We knelt down and literally washed the feet of our Buddhist brothers and sisters, that is, those who chose. There were twelve of them, as I remember. When William was washing Joseph Goldstein's feet— Jewish man, Buddhist practitioner, and founder of the Barre Center for Buddhist Studies in Massachusetts—I saw tears streaming down his face. He experienced the Christ at his feet. We were just washing feet—but through faith (and he would not have had our shared faith), the shared Christ-consciousness quickened his heart.

The same thing happened at Nuns in the West II in Hsi Lai Temple in Los Angeles, where there were Buddhist and Catholic nuns. We had a Mass in their ordination chapel. Here was this Jesuit, sitting in a lotus style, celebrating Mass, with this great Buddha be- hind him. It was awesome. The Christian nuns were sitting in the center and the Buddhist nuns were standing around. The Buddhists have 356 vows, and one of them is not to touch anyone. At the kiss of peace, we became *one.* The Catholic nuns turned around to the Buddhist nuns, the tears that flowed, the emotions that flowed be- tween us in that setting, the experience of being one in Buddha- nature, one in the Christ-consciousness, one in knowing that we are all sentient beings together in our lifetime—very specific, very alive, very conscious, very aware in those shared memories.

What is elemental about a community is the fact that it is vibrant with energies that could be put on a radar screen that is quickened, that is at a certain caliber that would sustain it. When one person is down, somebody else brings them up. When one person is up, she or he can bring somebody else up who is down. This energy or presence is actual. Christ Jesus is working through the community.

Community would have a few other aspects like membership and leadership.

Leadership

In leadership, cenobites are totally under the abbot and follow the Rule: basically, the Gospel is our guide, but the Rule particularizes it for us, especially the writings of the fathers, the conferences, the institutes, and earlier Rules. The abbot particularizes the teachings for the members, for he is believed to hold the place of Christ (RB 2.3). Whether he acts that way or she can sustain it—that is not the point. The point is that this pivotal person in the community is constitutive of what it means to be cenobitic: we are under an abbot, abbess, or prioress, meaning we are subservient or we bow or we use our energy because that person represents Christ to us. We accept direction: we consent and assent; we give that person the permission to exercise our muscle of faith, to quicken our faith, to make our faith stronger. It is about living as a faith community, that is, keeping this *koinonia* being as close a replica of the early church as we can and of being of service to others.

Membership

So, the leadership is enabled by the membership. In this membership there is a jealous lover. The cenobitic life is the primary community. The idea behind being cenobitic is that we are "no place else." The ring I was given at my final vows is the only ring that represents my commitment. My primary relationship is with Christ Jesus. The community represents Christ Jesus for me; they become my existential, primary group from which I work out my salvation and—lucky them—they get to use me for their salvation, God love them. The primacy or distinctiveness or actuality of this community, and no other community being a close second, is what the cenobitic idea is. We are not gyrovagues; we are not sarabaites; we are not hermits. We are cenobitic, which means we go together, we go as a community, but we go in faith because faith is constitutive. In order for my community to be primary, one of the elemental essentials is to live physically day by day, morning, noon, and night, with that same community. It is an environment, a stable place. *Stabilitas loci* is not a myth that does not have substance, which is not anchored without actuality. I live at Beech Grove. Now we come and we go, but only through obedience. To the extent that we are disobedient or we start creating other primary communities, we are straying from the elemental, that is, we are straying from that original call and we are diluting our Christ-consciousness. So, membership is essential.

Engagement, an aspect of membership

There are three distinctive characteristics of membership. First, there is engagement: we have to play our roles. We cannot just reside there; we cannot be in assisted living, an idea borrowed from Nancy, the prioress at Saint Benedict's Monastery. Our life is a faith life, so we cannot absent ourselves from this life of faith with its roles and engagement. What is that engagement? It is being on the spiritual journey, each one of us and all of us together.

Spiritual journey, second aspect of membership

The spiritual journey exists to sustain the renunciation. We renounce the world, the technical term for all that leads away from God. We renounce anything "away from God," and we are going toward God by using our primary community, our cenobitic community. The second renunciation[5] is to renounce our thoughts and my former way of life: food, sex, things, anger, dejection, *acedia*,

5. As I understand it, the error of the Messalians was that they sacralized ordinary motivations and actions without the right effort of *praktike*. There is no way other than ascetical work, with God's grace, to remove the false self. It is the true self that works unto faith, and we can trust that it is the Lord and not our afflictions at work unto death. The huge consequence of this distinction is that we must do our ascetical work of the second renunciation to be on the spiritual journey.

vainglory, and pride—those afflictions. To the extent we carry with us the affliction of anger, or of depression, or of overeating, or of overworking—whatever the affliction would be—it covers over our consciousness. To that extent, we are absenting ourselves from the community; we are not present; and we do not experience the Christ-presence that is available to us by virtue of our baptism and being in this community. These afflictions cost us a lot. We need to use our tools to reduce them and to move them out.

Third aspect of membership: lectio divina

Another distinguishing characteristic of a community is to do *lectio divina. Lectio divina* is the culture of a monastic community. If one reads Jean Leclercq's book *The Love of Learning and the Desire for God*[6] carefully, one sees what we are doing in the community. What are we doing in the bucket, but *lectio divina? Lectio divina* is the inner work that we are all doing, literally putting on the Scriptures by symbolically understanding them and moving into their myth systems. This is why we need beauty and architecture. This is why we need to open the senses of our aesthetics. *Lectio divina* goes deeper into the moral imperatives: we must do what those Scriptures call us to do. Then we have to open up and do the hard work of the ascetical life, which is to lay aside these afflictions and to replace them with ceaseless prayer. We cannot stay awake even in an awake community if we do not have inner practice, and that is what our silence practice is about. The fourth level of *lectio divina* is the mystical level, the union level. To sustain this, at some point we shift beyond right effort to no effort, where we let God be God, and God is alive and at work in our lives and we experience this presence to follow wherever that takes us by yielding to that energy.

---

6. Jean Leclercq, *The Love of Learning and the Desire for God: A Study of Monastic Culture*, trans. Catharine Misrahi (New York: Fordham University Press, 1961).

Part Two: Listening

The first of two poles is listening, but the technical language and teaching about listening in our tradition is under the practices of silence. Silence has three degrees. *The first degree is solitude*, where we enter into the cloister: we have times, places, spaces—the cell, enclosure—where we are alone with the Alone, our Beloved. These are the places where we can be in tune again with our Christ-consciousness. This point of silence, that is, solitude, we need to observe. The word "observance" is not bad.[7] In the Trappist reform, they saw that the monastics of that day had all the rhetoric but none of the action. In other words, they did not *do* it. Is that not the critique of traditionalists to us today? They see us with all the monastic buildings and places and language, but they are calling us out of mediocrity. They want us to be more intense and more fervent. So, they are starting new communities and new ways because they do not see it in us. In any event, the restart is through observance. We *do* the *horarium*, we *do* the rule of life, we *are* there and we *show up* at prayers, and we *observe*. In the pole of silence, we observe the cloister or our cell.

The second degree of silence is the practice of silence. What are we doing with our heart while we are in our cell? Now there are four classic ways to manage these afflictions when they come up.[8] What do we do when we are angry? What do we do when we are fantasizing off the wall of how great we are? The first way is just to observe, notice, *nepsis*, to keep vigil, step back and be present: "Oh, there it goes again. Um, I hope they clap." *Nepsis* handles about 80 percent of the afflictions of our thoughts and brings us back to this Christ-consciousness,

---

7. For more information on asceticism in the spiritual journey, see my three books: *Thoughts Matter* (1998), *Tools Matter* (2001), and *Humility Matters* (2005) (New York: Continuum International Publishing Group). My writings are catechetical in voice and are a redaction from translated sources.

8. If you want a reader-friendly scholarly study from original sources, see Columba Stewart's *Cassian the Monk* (New York: Oxford University Press, 1998). Or see Thomas Merton, *Cassian and the Fathers: Initiation into the Monastic Tradition*, Monastic Wisdom Series 1, ed. Patrick F. O'Connell (Kalamazoo, MI: Cistercian Publications, 2005).

that is, to this inner spaciousness of being. The elemental is *being*; it is what we experience that is bigger than any of us. It is the collectivity and manifestation of God, the mystery, the awesome, the presence. So, the first is *nepsis*, to watch, to observe, to just see, to wake before the dawn, to anticipate: "Oh, here it comes." So, we guard our thoughts: "Oh, I can't go there. I can't talk to that person."

The second one is to combat, where we take it on and say, "O God, come to my assistance." Or we say, "I am not a glutton. I am going to have more discipline in my life. I am going to do whatever it takes." Or there is the scriptural *antirrhesis*, a very serious thing in the desert tradition, where an elder would know in our heart what our affliction is and unlock that affliction by giving us a word. "Pray, father, give me a word that I may live." He would give a word and the word would open up that space in us that is afflicted, so that it neutralizes it and we come back to our default of Christ-consciousness. That is what *lectio divina* does.

The *third* practice is to literally watch our thoughts, guard our hearts, but also to have a *practice for our thoughts*, so as they rise, we not only notice them but we also replace that thought with another thought. One of the best thoughts to replace them with is a prayer. Of course, the tradition of the Jesus prayer would be to replace the thought with the name of Jesus, so that the name "Christ Jesus" is the thought in our hearts. In the elemental we want to be this consciousness of Jesus at all times. So, the third way is literally to pray without ceasing, that is, to have a prayer practice that is continuously at work in our hearts.

Now the *fourth* way is also very profound—that of *pure apostolic love*. This is where mission comes in for monastics: to *do* the Word of God with no thought of self. Selfless service annihilates, just totally scatters any darkness in our soul and brings us to the mystical moment of one Christ loving himself through our service. This is our tradition; this is the work we are doing in the monastery. This is why we have that pole of silence.

Taciturnity is for the sake of doing this inner work. We have a lot of work to do. We are doing one or another of these four practices while we are in the silence, while we are walking from here to there.

We need nightly silence to lay aside all the din that has happened between our ears all day long and get to that still place.

The third degree of silence is stillness of the body. This is where we sit in stillness, *hesychia*. We can go through our body to this Christ-consciousness, because frankly we are just made of light.[9] If we ever get still enough, it is our tradition that we can see our own inner light; if we are very still, our afflictions are subsided and the body is at rest in contemplation. There is a light and we are just in this presence. Yes, we are in the presence of Christ Jesus, but we too are an incarnate being; we too have a vibratory consciousness that is full of light. Each of us is made in the image and likeness, meaning the light, of God. This stillness is what this whole form is meant to bring us to, in between the psalms, as we go into church, *statio*, as we bow going out, as we listen to table reading, as we go to our cells, and as we work in the garden.

When we go back to our cells, as we go to sleep and as we commend ourselves with the words, "Accept me, O Lord, according to Thy word and I shall live," we sit or lie in that silence. Even if we do not know it by visual presence, we know it by faith: "I am in Christ Jesus. I am one." Through Christ Jesus we are one with the Trinity, which is this enormous energy of love, this presence of the Holy Spirit. This reign has begun, and it has begun in us; it is at work in us; it is bigger than we are. So, the purpose of silence and this whole solitude—the cloister and the inner practice of silence—is for the stillness: to experience this light and to bring this light[10] back up to

9. Evagrius has a systematic teaching on the spiritual journey: *Praktikos*, the *Gnostikos*, and the *Kephalaia Gnostica*. From the beginning in *praktike*, through the various levels of knowledge, to its goal in knowledge of the Holy Trinity, we see a road map to guide toward spiritual progress. In *Praktikos* the monk progresses through the eight principal temptations that afflict a monk and gains experience of passion-lessness. One of the signs of accessing *apatheia* is when the mind sees its own light at the time of prayer and is calm in the face of distractions. See Jeremy Driscoll, *Steps to Spiritual Perfection: Studies on Spiritual Progress in the Works of Evagrius* (New York: Newman Press, 2005), 23–24.

Another source for teachings on seeing one's own inner light is Columba Stewart, "Imageless Prayer and the Theological Vision of Evagrius Ponticus," *Journal of Early Christian Studies*, no. 9 (2001): 174–82.

10. Also, the teaching on one's own inner light is a corrective to a presumptuous assumption that I am already in the unitive stage. A second caution is to guard against

suscipe: "I'll do whatever you want. What is it you will have me do? Here I am, Lord." This is our call from mission, which we do selflessly under obedience and together with the community, where we abandon ourselves.

Part Three: Hospitality

The next pole obviously is hospitality. If we have experienced the silence, if we have experienced in the seeking of God this moment of presence, it is very natural for us to want to use our monastic, community forms to invite others. We do not really have to invite anybody; they will come. They see this light; they experience this attraction; they want to be where we are; and they want to taste it. They do not have language for it, but they know it and we know it, too. We are so blessed. They also know when we are full of affliction and we are emanating affliction. So, we must reduce those afflictions of a group and individually, because they are in the way of our elemental monastic way of life. Can they also be the way? Very much so! On the other side of those afflictions is this stillness, this repentance, this reconciliation that we rely totally on God.

Hospitality also has three degrees of seriousness. *The first degree would be providing a safe space,* a convening like Saint Benedict's community did for us. We came into their campus; they showed us what was going on there; they invited us into their dining room and into their worship. The sisters were welcoming and we had many conversations. We were there all day; it was just a lovely, lovely event. So, hospitality is a safe, spacious space, warm, welcoming, and interactive.

---

uncritically appropriating the advaidic, nondual experience available to those beyond the purgative phases of the spiritual journey. It seems that God's love is unconditional, but from the human side we do not experience it if we are in the grip of the afflictions. The teaching on inner light is given here with caution. It would be against humility to have one's mind fixed on outcomes in prayer!

There is a pejorative usage of the word "duality," meaning two. The Christian duality is not a term to foster oppositional duality as in patriarchy or some denial of the body as in Gnosticism. The Creator and the creature are in a loving relationship. Perhaps it would be better to use the word "dyad," but the creature isn't peer to the Creator. Hence, we incur the language difficulty.

This safe, spacious place also has boundaries, so that we would always remain in our skin. Gregory the Great talks about Benedict being "self-possessed," meaning he lived in his own skin. Our monasteries have to be who we are, and we have a distinctive vowed formula that there are differential degrees of membership. The vowed core members have a different space. It is like dialogue. If we do not keep our space sacred and come to the welcoming space, then there is nothing to say. In dialogue, if we do not come from center to center, there is going to be no dialogue. The same is true of hospitality. We have to keep our cloister, our refectories, and our cells. Benedict provided for that. He had a guest master, the porter, the abbot's table, and times and places for the visitors. We need to have that, too, in order for this to work. That is the dynamics, the elemental. We are not a crowd; we are not a group; we are not an ideological mission statement.

The second degree of hospitality is much more difficult. It is *the reciprocity of the mutuality* of the people who come to us. We interact; we become friends: they know us and we know them. We become available for them; we do what we can for them; we serve them, and we also accept their invitation to collaborate on this and that. It is a very rigorous dialogue and practice—this reciprocity and mutuality. It is not just receiving them; it certainly is not a formal dining room, where everyone bows and everyone has a seat and we have chamber music. To work out the details is to keep the boundaries.

The third degree of hospitality addresses: "What is going on in your mind when you do hospitality? How can we be reciprocal?" We have to be *open and welcoming in our inner conversation.* We cannot be saying, "Oh, I am going to use him. I think he could give us some money." Or, "I don't like him. I sure hope he doesn't come back." Or, "I'm not home." My father had an office with a back door and a back stairway. Many a time I asked, "Where's Dad?" "Oh, he went out the back way." We do not have a back door, but we can send somebody else who is more extroverted. More important in hospitality is to ask, "What are we doing with our mind?" We cannot judge; we cannot be harsh; we cannot be critical. Remember what Peregrine stated, "There's Christ at the door!" Oh, yes, "Jesus Christ, it's you again!" That is faith at work in our midst. It is not only to do the behaviors.

It is like silence, where it is not good just to observe silence. We have to do the inner work of practice. In hospitality the inner work is to create that spaciousness in our hearts where guests are welcome to the level of their need. "Yes, I've got time. Sit down." Or, "I don't have time, but let's talk about it another time." So, it is about a whole exchange and to be open to whoever they are and how they are, to let them feed us and we feed them; it is a marvelous exchange of the *koinonia*.

This third level is beyond the practices of the mind. It is to be willing to sacrifice for the sake of another; it stands the test of time, like picking up someone at the airport. The community, because it is our primary community, has total claim on our time, so, if we are sent, that is Christ Jesus sending us to Christ Jesus. So, there is some kind of exchange here that we know not what. To be willing to sacrifice is more that just comfort and the business of hospitality.

As an example of this inner hospitality there is the story of Dom Christian de Chergé. He was one of the monks of Atlas who was murdered by very fundamentalist Muslims in Algiers ten years ago. Eleven years ago I was giving a report to the DIM, the international board for interreligious dialogue, and Dom de Chergé was giving his report on Algiers. He was talking about Muslim dialogue; he was impassioned, and he asked me what I was doing for Muslim dialogue. He had this fire in his eyes; he was just an amazing monk who was challenging us, because up until now we had been doing dialogue mainly with our monastic counterparts—Buddhists, Hindus, maybe Sufis. As is well known, that monastery and those seven monks had to make a choice to "stay in place." They had given part of their property for a mosque because there was so much terrorist activity that the local Muslims needed a place to pray five times a day. So, they had the call to prayer for the Trappist house and a call to prayer for the Muslims right there on the property. One of the monks, a doctor, had a little clinic for all the Muslims in the area. It was very apparent to them that they were at risk, for there were many murders happening around them. The Trappists had a meeting to discuss: "Was this suicide or soul-cide? Were they really giving their souls and staying in place and being in service, or was this suicidal, or is it martyrdom to stay there?" They decided to "stay in place." Hospitality was to stay in place, to be of comfort, to be of service to those Muslims in that area. This is more than meets the eye, for they learned Arabic, they learned about their prayers, and they learned more about the Qur'an. They had a sustained dialogue with their neighbors with lots of mystery between them. Mystery here means "let's stand at the whole intelligibility of Allah and the Muslim way of life compared to the Christian way of life of Christ Jesus. Let the differences stand and be present to one another and humanly to be open to each other." This understanding was shared at the Gethsemani Encounter I, which was in June of that year.

This past July ten years ago this week we had Gethsemani Encounter II, where Dom Armand Veilleux, one of the superiors of the Trappists, and Bernardo Olivera, the abbot general, claimed that they got the heads, not the bodies, back. It is an actual fact that Dom Christian sent to his family his testimonial of what he thought he was doing there.[11] It is a classic piece of literature and prayer. He said things like, "I envision my executioner and we are like the two men crucified on either side of Christ and we will be taken up into heaven together as brothers, *en-visagé*: I see your face and face-to-face we come. And I forgive you and I hope you forgive me." This was a total reconciliation and willingness to stay in place for the sake of those Muslim neighbors. There are many stories around these events, but the energy and Christ-consciousness in that very place now is that it is like a shrine. Francis Kline, OCSO, told me that the toaster is still plugged in. The Muslims in that area will not let anybody in. It is just a hallowed place because these monks gave their life for them. Our Trappist brothers and sisters and those who have given their lives are right there ahead of us and helping us stay in place, helping us to remove the obstacles to our Christ-consciousness.

---

11. See the translation of the English version of the testimonial of Dom Christian de Chergé at the following web site: http://www.ocso.org/testc-vv.htm#Testament.

Part Four: Humility

Humility is that wheel that keeps us on the ground, sometimes moves us, sometimes parks us, and keeps the burden of community squarely on top of us, where we are poised, ready, and willing. Humility is simply the reverse side of the four renunciations: when our former way of life is rooted out, and our afflictions cease to dominate our consciousness. Purity of heart replaces gluttony, lust, greed, anger, depression, *acedia*, vainglory, and pride. Instead, these are replaced by humility. Enlightenment for a Christian—one will know it when one sees it by their humility. Brief moments of illumination manifest as the "I Am," and not in some idol of our imagination or self-made mental constructs. If our minds are foggy we crash into one vicissitude after another. If we monastics embark seriously on the monastic way of life, moving through the four renunciations, then our faith will sustain us. We relax into the stillness of our own light; our minds clear and we shift from self to sacrifice easily with the grace of God. It is not hard when we are not doing it. That wheel is just moving along. It is not a burden. Everything is balanced, poised, ready, conscious, and active.

Humility provides the direction, the focus, and the energy that enable us to journey through life with gratitude. Grace is the lubricant that smooths the way before us. The burden of a balanced load of listening and hospitality is safely carried over the wheel of humility. Every community has its own dynamics, but when energized by humility there is a fresh and quick spirit voiced at our Liturgy of the Hours.

As Christians we can do no better than follow the teachings, example, words, and deeds of Jesus. What is certain is that it is through being human that we are saved. We need not shift into higher states of consciousness, become perfect, or proficient, or even reach our final incarnation. We have been freed from our sins in Christ Jesus. He has redeemed us and calls us to repent of personal sin, so that if we are willing and humble enough to accept his gift, everything is done for us. In humility we bow down, filled with compunction and ready to go where he goes and to follow the impulses of the Holy Spirit to those ever-new reigns of glory and grace.

Conclusion

If the wheelbarrow of community has balanced loads of hospitality and silence, it sits steady and stable on the wheel of humility. The elemental form of a monastery makes accessible the Mystery; the Mystery of God's Presence is accessible, right here, right now. The classic form keeps the monastics faithful to vocation. Here are a few examples of four elemental themes I have witnessed from my travels:

- Despite the huge numbers who flock to Gethsemani, the monks still wash every dish after every meal of all the guests who pass through year after year, honoring Merton's legacy.

- The new monastery at Saint Mary's in Rock Island fosters solitude on the edge of the city, and they have downsized to be just the right size in beauty and elegance. They point to the elemental for their way of life right now.

- At Clyde, Missouri, those nuns actively strive for praxis in silence, not just the practice of silence; they have an inner work that they are doing, walking here and there within the cloister.

- At Fort Smith, when I was there for a Novice Institute a couple of years ago, I encountered a community where no unkind word was spoken about another. I knew something bad about someone, so at table I asked, "How is sister so and so?" "Oh, she is just fine; she's doing this and this." There was not an unkind word at Fort Smith in a whole week.

- The nuns at Ridgley, Maryland, provide selfless service to those whom society tends to ignore and to families that cannot manage with their limited resources. They have an orphanage situation, and a school for the handicapped, and resident homes for retarded adults.

- At Redwoods Trappistine Abbey, they close their guest facilities for three months every year to provide time for the community to be alone. They make solitude the whole place, where they practice the silence and become still in the Redwoods. Is that not awesome? To wake up and know that there is a group of nuns in their stillness is something! I get thrilled when I go to a Trappist monastery and know that those monks at three o'clock are doing Vigils for the sake of all of us.

- Saint Meinrad, Conception Abbey, and Gethsemani Abbey all have new welcome centers to enable them to cope with the flow of visitors, while maintaining the integrity of the monastic way of life for their monks.

- At Annunciation Monastery in Bismarck, North Dakota, they have downsized to fit their size. They sold their old monastery to the university and built a new monastery that architecturally shapes them with beauty and grace. On my way to prayers I saw that the blue in the windows is the same blue as the North Dakota sky; it is not a blue we have in Indiana.

More could be added to this list. Like a simple, serviceable wheelbarrow, if we remain faithful to our tradition of community, silence, hospitality, and humility, then the next generation after us will experience the Mystery of God's Presence.

Responders to Mary Margaret (Meg) Funk, OSB

*Gerald Schlabach, Kathy Berken,
Dorothy Bass, Craig Wood, Brian Terrell*

Each of five responders to Mary Margaret Funk's presentation represented a form of intentional community, whose purpose is to live in Christian discipleship.

Gerald Schlabach:[1] I represent Bridgefolk, which is about bridging—transcending old polarities, exchanging and integrating the gifts of mutually "separated brethren" and sisters, too. It is about imagining Christ's church without the divisions that long seemed to be givens, and doing the next thing God gives us to do in order that this vision might become reality. Many of those next things that we seek to bridge are evident in the lead paragraph of our mission statement:

> Bridgefolk is a movement of sacramentally-minded Mennonites and peace-minded Roman Catholics who come together to celebrate each other's traditions, explore each other's practices, and honor

---

1. Gerald Schlabach is professor of theology at the University of Saint Thomas, Saint Paul, Minnesota. In the 1980s Professor Schlabach did some work with the Mennonite Central Committee in Nicaragua and Honduras; he has written several books about peacemaking and the Gospel. In 1997 he became a Benedictine oblate; in 1999 he helped to convene a group of Mennonites and Catholics who were interested in exploring each others' traditions. That group is now called Bridgefolk.

each other's contribution to the mission of Christ's Church. Together we seek better ways to embody a commitment to both traditions. We seek to make Anabaptist-Mennonite practices of discipleship, peaceableness, and lay participation more accessible to Roman Catholics, and to bring the spiritual, liturgical, and sacramental practices of the Catholic tradition to Anabaptists.[2]

In order to explain what this has to do with either monasticism or "new monasticism," and how Bridgefolk can have something to do with both when it is not a *local* community, and its only slender "rule" is a single common prayer, we would do well to recognize that tensions exist between the four Benedictine values that Sister Joan Chittister names, as well as others she might name.[3]

These tensions are a good thing, that is, they are creative, not tragic, ones. To name these tensions is not to criticize either her or the Benedictine tradition. Much less are they grounds for discouragement. For it is in holding these tensions together that all of us—classic monastics and new monastics, professed and lay, oblates and seekers—will generate what we most have to offer the church and the world.

Sister Meg has already discussed the tensions between *community* and *hospitality* very well. To negotiate this abiding but creative tension, *humility* and *listening*—the other two Benedictine values that Chittister names—prove all the more important. Yet here too we must note creative tensions. We all know that leaders can abuse the humility of those with less power, and often do so precisely in the name of community.

Perhaps listening is not directly in tension with the other three Benedictine values, but the very practice of attentive listening may initially accentuate tensions. "Listening to the Word of God, to the tradition, to one another, to the circumstances of life becomes the cornerstone of spiritual growth," writes Chittister.[4] Yes! One does

---

2. Mission Statement of Bridgefolk, available at: http://bridgefolk.net.

3. Joan Chittister, OSB, "And He Shall Be Called," *National Catholic Reporter Online* (April 20, 2005); http://www.nationalcatholicreporter.org/update/conclave/jc042005.htm.

4. Ibid., page 2 of printout of the web page.

not need to listen long to either the testimony of church history or the noise of contemporary debates to hear Christians pitting one or another of the sources on that list against the others!

Here is where we see the deeper contribution that Bridgefolk hopes to make, though of course not uniquely. While we most obviously seek to help build a bridge between Mennonite peacemaking traditions and Catholic sacramental traditions, *any* rapprochement between these churches represents hope for *another* bridge—between Christian impulses of prophetic dissent, which took archetypical shape in the sixteenth-century Radical Reformation, and Christian commitments to apostolic community, which take archetypical shape in Roman Catholicism.

The need and value of this bridge is present in Chittister's article in one obvious way and in another unnoticed one. Its obvious context—indeed the subject of its entire first half of the article—was anxiety about Cardinal Ratzinger becoming Pope Benedict XVI, given the cardinal's reputation as a stern authoritarian. Unnoticed and unnamed, however, is another Benedictine value.

That value is stable monastic rootedness in the sacramental life of the church, through the continuous rhythm of liturgical prayer and eucharistic sharing. This further Benedictine value is so basic that Chittister apparently took it for granted. But by juxtaposing the Anabaptist/Mennonite tradition with the Roman Catholic tradition, Bridgefolk offers a reminder that to overlook it is a mistake. Efforts at church renewal—calling individual Christians to more fervent discipleship and Christian communities to greater faithfulness—have regularly enough led to alienation from church structures and ruptures in Christian communion that we ought to underscore so as not to overlook this value.

However, not all Bridgefolk participants would immediately name the bridging of prophetic dissent and apostolic continuity as our charism. But if we are contributing in any lasting way to Mennonite/Catholic reconciliation, in whatever form that might take in the future, this could be Bridgefolk's greatest historical significance: affirming that movements for church renewal and prophetic dissent ought rightly to contribute to the catholic whole rather than breaking with the whole.

In a way, this continuity—this bridge—is nothing more than the vow of stability and the virtue of fidelity writ large. Sister Joan represents it in her own way by courageously dissenting, while being doggedly loyal to the church. Monasticism, in its long arc of working for Christian renewal, but praying the prayers of the church, represents that bridge in another way. Amid culture wars and clashes of civilization so-called, however, this is a witness that the church, civil society, and a globalizing world all desperately need. As such, it is nothing to take for granted.

Most of this message is probably directed to the "new monastic" movements of various sorts, in terms of the value of keeping connected to the larger church. Here are a few more remarks directed toward old or classic monastics.

Sister Meg said that if the "wheelbarrow" is balanced with all the basic elements and the elemental form, this will make clear the mystery. Celibacy was not one of the things mentioned as an elemental form, and yet most historians and observers would say that it is basic to monasticism.

Now the Anabaptist Mennonite tradition, as my colleague Ivan Kauffman says, "The sixteenth-century Anabaptist-Mennonite tradition is the *old* 'new monasticism.'" That impulse, already in the sixteenth century, growing out of late medieval movements and so connected with the deeper tradition, is saying, "We want to be able to live the kind of life that has been available classically in monasteries, but we want to live it as married people. It is not because we can't control our desires and just have to get married, but because Jesus Christ calls all of us to serious lives of discipleship."

Part of what Bridgefolk represents, and what attracts Mennonites, is reconnecting that kind of life they already have to the sacramental, longer, classic traditions, but for Catholics (I am speaking now as a Mennonite Catholic), what they see in Mennonites is that possibility still again that we too can live a serious kind of Christian life, intentionally following Christ in the totality of our lives in the world. So, the big question to get on the table is: What about the experiments of combining married life and celibate life in an integrated community? What are the possibilities? What are the problems?

Kathy Berken:[5] I was really pleased that Sister Meg was speaking about the mystery of God's presence because I am going to tell you two stories. But first of all, Jean Vanier, in case you do not know, is our founder, who in 1964 took two men out of an institution in France and decided to live a more humane life with them in a religious community in a home. The word spread, and now after forty-two years there are one hundred thirty-three L'Arche communities in the world, in thirty-three countries.

My community in Clinton, Iowa, has three homes, and we have an apartment community with five core members, so a total of nineteen "core members," which is the name of the people with disabilities, and the rest of us who help and live there are "assistants." I live in one of the homes and I am the House Coordinator of that home. Here are my two stories.

Mass at the Canticle[6]

When I first came to Clinton, Iowa, in October 1999, Jean Vanier was visiting us for our twenty-fifth anniversary. We were all at The Canticle—the motherhouse for the Clinton Franciscan Sisters—for Sunday Mass with all the core members and Jean Vanier. When the priest held up the bread and wine at Mass and said the words of consecration, "This is my Body, broken for you. This is my Blood, shed for you," I thought about the core members around me, and I felt grateful that God gave them to me in this way, as broken bodies.

I felt blessed, truly and inexplicably blessed, to be called to L'Arche to serve God and discover what mysteries lay ahead for me.

The Body of Christ was here somewhere. Transubstantiation. *Koinonia.*

---

5. Kathy C. Berken is currently the House Coordinator for the L'Arche Community in Clinton, Iowa, where she is responsible for five men with developmental (cognitive) disabilities. She was also a L'Arche assistant since 1999. She recently published a book on her experiences with the L'Arche Community entitled *Walking on a Rolling Deck: Life on the Ark* (Collegeville, MN: Liturgical Press, 2008).

6. A variation of this story appears in Kathy's book, *Walking on a Rolling Deck: Life on the Ark*, 65–66.

Exactly one year later, in October 2000, I was at The Canticle again for Mass with the core members from our house. This time, however, was radically different. I had just had surgery for stage IV breast cancer less than two weeks previous. I wore a sixteen-inch-long, five-inch-wide bandage across my chest. There were two foot-long drainage tubes still inside me attached to plastic bottles that looked like little hand grenades, which were hanging from my side and attached to a little pouch I wore around my waist. I was scheduled to begin eighteen weeks of chemotherapy in a few days.

When the priest said the words of consecration that morning, I heard them with different ears and a different heart. Mysteries about why I was in this L'Arche community began to unfold. I felt that now my body was broken and blood was being poured out, not for me, but for them. The core members and other members of this L'Arche community would be caring for me for a while. The line was blurred between who was broken—if, indeed any of us really were—and why. If there was brokenness, at least of body, we were broken for each other. I discovered this.

This was God's community. This was God's gift of L'Arche. We were the Mystical Body of Christ and this was Eucharist.

Roberta and Christmas Morning[7]

My second story involves Roberta, a core member, who is pictured walking across the finishing line with her housemate in the brochure of our community. We lived in a different house together when I first came to L'Arche, so this story also involves my first year in the community.

My first Christmas at L'Arche in 1999 started out awful. I was homesick. It was the first Christmas ever that I was not spending with my family. I was especially lonely for Christmas pasts of special breakfasts of eggs, sausage, and homemade coffee cake. Here I was told to fend for myself as we were invited to another house for turkey dinner a little bit later. I faced the grim reality and I was *not* happy.

7. See ibid., 27–29, where the story is entitled, "Christmas Morning with Gertie."

I headed to the kitchen where I spotted a pot of leftover bean soup on the stove. That, I decided, was going to be my breakfast. Just then, Roberta stopped me. "Kathy, I want to show you something," she said. Roberta is a four-foot-tall, sixty-year-old core member with Down syndrome who is hard of hearing and has no teeth. On the table were my favorite dishes, some cottage cheese, a plate of toast, my favorite mug filled with water, a jelly glass with orange juice, butter, a knife, and spoon.

Roberta's face was glowing. She said, "I made you breakfast!" She swept her arm back as if to make a presentation, and added, "I did this all for you." I sat down across from her. All I could do was stare. I mixed some cottage cheese with applesauce and spread some butter on the toast, which by now was cold and hard, but she didn't know that and I didn't care. She said, "I am serving you now."

I glanced out the window at the snow on the evergreen bushes and the sun was shining and it was Christmas morning. I never told anyone my self-pitying history, let alone Roberta. She had never made me breakfast before this and she has never made me breakfast since.

When I looked down at my plate, I could hardly see my food. As I finished various parts of my meal, Roberta would get up and stand by me and ask, "Are you done?" And she would take the empty dish to the sink, return, and wait. I finished everything on my plate. It didn't matter if I might not be hungry for a turkey dinner in two hours. A friend with a huge heart, who gives more hugs than any person clinically needs in a day, had gifted me.

I saw God that day and God fed me. If this wasn't Eucharist and the "real presence" of Jesus Christ, then I'm not sure where to look for it.

Dorothy Bass:[8] I will tell you about what Holden is, since it is probably less familiar than some of the other communities repre-

8. Dorothy Bass directs the Valparaiso Project on the Education and Formation of People in Faith (www.practicingourfaith.org), a Lilly Endowment project at Valparaiso University, and is the author of several books: *Practicing our Faith: A Way of Life for a Searching People*; *Receiving the Day: Christian Practices for Opening the Gift*

sented here, before moving on to a theological point about community, which I have learned at Holden and hope may also be relevant to your communities in some way.

Holden Village is a place, a cluster of Swiss-looking buildings nestled in a stunningly beautiful alpine valley in the north Cascades. It was constructed for a copper mining operation in 1937 and donated to a Lutheran organization in 1961. The only ways to get in there is to hike in for three days over several mountain passes, or the way most of us go is to take an eleven-mile bus ride over a narrow gravel road from a lakeside dock, which itself is a three-hour boat ride from the nearest town.

Holden Village is also a way of life, shaped by an ongoing but constantly evolving set of practices. Foremost among these is daily Vespers: thirty-minute services for six nights of the week and a great, lavish Eucharist on Sunday. Occasionally grace erupts and our worship is what Holden's leaders hope and proclaim, the source and summit of our life together. Other practices that are distinctive arise from concern for the environment and global economic justice. For example, we live simply, eat low on the food chain, recycle assiduously—no big deal perhaps, but a surprise and challenge to many guests and a spur to how we live once we get back home. Holden's way of life also incorporates lively learning and conversation, which are always in summer and often in winter energized by volunteer theologians, and artists, and spiritual directors.

Third, Holden is a ministry, a gathering of people and resources that exists not for its own sake, but for the sake of the church and the world. Daniel Erlander, a former Village pastor, calls Holden a "wilderness school," an echo of the school in which the children of Israel wandered for forty years as they slowly shed the patterns of enslavement and learned the rhythms of freedom. Holden's mission is to send villagers back down the mountain to be salt and yeast in their own contexts.

---

of Time; Practicing Theology: Beliefs and Practices in Christian Life; and *Way to Live: Christian Practices for Teens*. Dorothy serves on the board of directors for Holden Village, an ecumenical retreat center in the northern Cascade Mountains.

So, Holden is a place, a way of life, a ministry, but is it a community? I can only offer a tentative, ambiguous "yes, but." Yes, but not in the way that a monastery or other stable household is and not in the same degree for all Villagers. I imagine what is going on there today. There are probably four hundred thirty people there, which is full summer capacity. Of these perhaps two hundred eighty are paying guests and one hundred fifty are staff members. Most of those staff members this time of year are short-term volunteers, perhaps college students or midlife people or retirees, many of whom return year after year for a time of renewal. Some are also long-term staff members who have spent the winter there together, having made at least a one-year commitment, though rarely more than two, as carpenter, cook, pastor, bookkeeper, whatever. About seventy of those long-termers, including their children, who attend a K-through-12 public school at Holden, have probably bonded and have come to think of the Village as their own during the quiet, delightful winter months. At this moment, I am sure that some of these are struggling to extend hospitality to the invading hordes of summer people, while others are really delighted to find their community enlivened and expanded by so many newcomers.

Different people experience Holden in different ways. No one stays at Holden permanently, so, in a sense, all of us who have experienced Christian formation there over time are oblates, not cenobites. I am drawing on my own experience over twenty-three years as a guest, staff, and board member. During this period Holden has remained surprisingly the same and also surprisingly different each time, while undergoing significant fluctuations of emphasis over time, depending on the leadership of directors, pastors, and longtime staff, who are there at that particular time. Frankly most of these fluctuations seem to me to be about our understanding of what is theologically central to our life together. This is something that must be continually reaffirmed, because Holden is a community that exists on the margin of the church in its geographic location and in its special openness to young people and those in transition. Also, as a Protestant community, a Lutheran ministry, we have no magisterium and no vow of obedience. So, in a sense, we are much like American culture itself for Protestants and the majority of lay Catholics alike, though we do have a strong theological tradition to draw on—the Lutheran theology of the cross. When we get things right, I think it is when we remember that theology.

Hospitality to those in transition or unsure of what to do in life has been an important part of Holden's ministry for more than forty years. Often these people are unsure about God, and perhaps especially about God's crucified and risen Son. They are also unsure about their relationship with others, though they are somehow drawn to a place that celebrates God's presence and values community. I am generalizing about groups of people across a wide spectrum. Added to this fact is that Holden is in the least churched region of our country—the Pacific Northwest—and it truly welcomes those shunned by many other Christians such as those who are divorced or gay. We find at any given time that some people are lifelong churchgoers with firm baptismal identities, and some are hovering mistrustfully on the outer boundaries of the church. And many, of course, are somewhere in between.

Drawing on the work of the liturgical theologian Gordon Lathrop, Village pastor Ben Stewart introduced the phrase into Village life a few years ago that articulates both deep hopes for the church as a whole (in a time we need to be thinking about evangelization), and also offers an image of Holden at its best. This phrase is "strong center, open door." The strong center is Jesus Christ, indeed Christ crucified, the one who knows the sin and brokenness of both the lifelong churchgoer and the wary seeker, the one who sees beyond and transforms the doctrinaire smugness of the former and the deconstructive suspicions of the latter. To claim a strong center means proclaiming the mercy, the unconditional love of this one in straightforward biblical terms, and doing our best to live that out. To offer an open door means trusting that this mercy is offered by God even to those who seem to criticize the institutional church that some of us love with every other breath. Beneath the cross both the supposedly righteous and the supposedly unrighteous are already welcomed, embraced, reconciled, and wrapped in the righteousness of Christ, not of their own. Dietrich Bonhoeffer puts it this way: "Christian

Community is not an ideal we have to realize, but rather a reality created by God in Christ, in which we may participate."[9]

Because Holden is beautiful and fun, rhythmic and accepting, and no one's permanent home, it readily can become a dream of community, and it readily becomes that for me sometimes, rather than the reality of Christian community itself. Ah, the dream suggests: "Here, away from the pressures of society, we can finally get it right." During an argument last year that arose after we had once again proven our inability to embody such a dream, a wise woman called our attention to a poignant, piercing passage from Bonhoeffer's little classic on Christian community, *Life Together*:

> On innumerable occasions a whole Christian community has been shattered because it has lived on the basis of a wishful image. Certainly serious Christians who are put in a community for the first time will often bring with them a very definite image of what Christian communal life . . . should be, and they will be anxious to realize it. [Anxiety is not good for community either.] But God's grace quickly frustrates all such dreams. . . . By sheer grace God will not permit us to live in a dream world even for a few weeks and to abandon ourselves to those blissful experiences and exalted moods that sweep over us like a wave of rapture. For God is not a God of emotionalism, but the God of truth.[10]

The problem with wishful dreaming—and this is very relevant to what Sister Meg stated—is that "it makes the dreamer proud and pretentious,"[11] and erodes the humility that allows us to see ourselves and one another truly, as utterly dependent on God and also as bearers of God's grace to and for one another.

In Lutheran terms, community becomes the demand of a law that we can never fulfill, rather than a gift of God, communicated through the Gospel and thankfully received by grace through faith.

---

9. Dietrich Bonhoeffer, *Life Together*, Dietrich Bonhoeffer Works, Volume 5: Life Together, Prayerbook of the Bible, trans. Daniel W. Bloesch and James H. Burtness (Minneapolis: Fortress Press, 1996), 38.

10. Ibid., 35.

11. Ibid., 36.

My experience at Holden suggests that community can thrive only when we turn again and again to the strong center, the cross of Christ, in which we are reconciled. At the same time, it reminds me that what we humbly and thankfully receive in Christ Jesus is given in order that it may be given away, for the sake of the whole world beloved by God, through a door that is always open, both at Holden and in our down-lake lives to which all Villagers eventually return.

Craig Wood:[12] The image of the wheelbarrow reminded me of what the apostle Paul says in 2 Corinthians, "But we have this treasure in clay jars" (2 Cor 4:7), and this is a great picture of what Paul is saying there. Christian life is supposed to be ordinary; Christians are a little beat up and sometimes neglected and taken for granted.

The Community of Sant'Egidio is not a Benedictine community, but it has been greatly influenced by Benedictine values. The Rule of Benedict was an important and formative influence on the community, and Benedictines have been a big influence on the community. Abbot Primate Wolf has been a good friend of the community from the very beginning. There have been other Benedictines who have had an influence on us.

Of these four terms or concepts of Benedictine monasticism we obviously use "community" a lot because we are not a residential community; we do not live together and we do not share stuff together. We are constantly reminding ourselves that we are a community. We are a community of people united in a common goal. We come together in prayer. We pray together as friends and we serve the poor together as friends. That is what our community is. So, we use the word "community" a lot. In fact, in the beginning we were known as "The Community" in the first five years of existence. It was not until they had to go to a conference somewhere and identify themselves as

12. Craig Wood is married with four children and four grandchildren and is an air traffic controller in Minneapolis and an oblate at Saint John's. He also has established the Community of Sant'Egidio that has met monthly since about January 2002, which has direct service to the elderly in Minneapolis. To learn more about this community, see its web site: http://www.santegidiousa.org, which has a link to its beginning group in Rome, Comunità di Sant'Egidio: http://www.santegidio.org.

to who they were that they had to come up with a more specific name. So, they said, "We're praying in the Church of Sant'Egidio, so why don't we call ourselves The Community of Sant'Egidio?"

While Meg talked about community in terms of membership and leadership, Sant'Egidio uses the model of friendship. Certainly there are leaders in our community and there are members, but we really look at ourselves as friends. We gather in friendship, which is a big concept for us. The other three terms—listening, humility, and hospitality—are not terms we explicitly use and talk about, other than listening, but they are included in what we talk about as friendship. The ideal of our community is that each day the members spend personal time listening to the Scriptures. Jesus called his disciples, "I have called you friends" (John 15:15). When we approach the Scriptures and when we pray, we are praying to our friend and we are listening for a word from our friend. When we gather together for our communal prayer, we gather as friends to listen to our friend. Our prayer is deeply rooted in Scripture and the tradition of the church.

It is important for us to listen not only to the Word but to one another and even more important to the world: what is the world saying? From the very beginning, one of the hallmarks of the community has been that the things the members have gotten involved in concern the world. They did not sit down and say, "Well, let's start a group that will hold an annual prayer for peace; let's mediate a peace agreement with Mozambique; let's have a soup kitchen; let's mentor gypsy children." They did not really have an agenda, but what they did was to go out and try to become friends with the poor and the weak, people who had needs. When they saw what the needs were there, they tried to meet those needs. They tried to serve the people, not as the more powerful to the weak, but as friends.

Hospitality, as Meg pointed out, means reciprocity and mutuality, which are important aspects of community. Most people who serve the poor and the weak have to talk about the fact that it is reciprocity and mutual; it is not the more powerful condescending to the weaker. In our community we use the word friendship to describe that reality. Friends are persons who are very hospitable, who have an open space in their lives for others, and have a welcoming spirit.

Meg talked about humility. Ultimately, one of the marks of good friends is that good friends are willing to set aside their own stuff to listen to your stuff, to be involved in your stuff, and be interested in your stuff. Humility under the guise of friendship is a very important thing.

The communities have a couple of big things they do, which everyone sees: the annual prayer for peace, which is obviously an expression of our willingness to listen to people who have different religious views than we do, to talk with them and dialogue, to welcome them and be hospitable to them. The peace agreement at Mozambique really arose out of this listening process and also from this need to help a friend. Even though the community does not use specifically a language of listening, humility, and hospitality, and so on, these are included in what we understand by friendship.

Brian Terrell:[13] I am here by accident or by default, as a last-minute stand-in for Frank Cordero, who was scheduled to speak on the Catholic Worker. Frank cannot be here because he is in jail, and so are our many Catholic Worker brothers and sisters these days, witnessing for peace in this country that is bent on war.

Jonathan Wilson-Hartgrove has already offered to us that jail can be an ascetical practice. Dorothy Day, cofounder of the Catholic Worker, who was also an oblate, often suggested to us, her younger coworkers, that we do something to get ourselves put in jail, as a nice "retreat." The theologian Jim Douglas argued that the *true* desert in modern America, the place where one might find true poverty of self and abandon oneself to God and to prayer, is not the monastery anymore, but the jail. "As we join the poor in jail," he wrote, "and deepen in our own poverty, continuing to respond in truth to the violence and injustice around us, the power of God will become real."[14]

---

13. Brian Terrell and his wife Betsy have a Catholic Worker House in Maloy, a little town in southern Iowa about forty miles from the monastery at Clyde, where they are oblates. Their place at Maloy is called Strangers and Guests Catholic Worker Farm.

14. James Douglas, "And I will seek God alone in the Wilderness," *The Catholic Agitator* 10, no. 9 (November 1980): 2.

Dorothy Day would laugh if she heard herself being offered as an exemplar of humility. As a young man I lived with Dorothy in her last years in community, and I can attest that the virtue of humility presented a lifelong challenge to her. Sometimes, though, she got it right.

Robert Coles, author, child psychiatrist, professor at Harvard, tells of his first meeting with Dorothy. Arriving at the Catholic Worker House of Hospitality on New York's Lower East Side, looking like the Harvard scholar that he was, he found Dorothy deep in conversation with a woman whom he described as drunk and filthy, with her own belongings scattered around her in shopping bags. Dorothy did not seem to notice Coles when he came in. Coles was standing there and finally he cleared his throat and Dorothy looked up and said, "Are you waiting to talk with one of us?"[15]

"Are you waiting to talk with one of us?"

In humility, Dorothy did not presume that she was any more worth seeking out and any more worth talking to than the next person; there was no presumption that she was more important or that her opinions would have more value than that of a woman who lived in the street.

I wondered when I read that story if she learned that from her times in jail. The labor leader Eugene Debs learned this monastic virtue when he was serving time during World War I under the Sedition Act. It occurred to him that he had kinship with all living things when he says, "I made up my mind that I am not one bit better than the meanest on earth." He said this: "While there is a lower class, I am in it. While there is a criminal element, I am of it and while there is a soul in prison, I am not free!"[16]

---

15. Robert Coles, *Dorothy Day: A Radical Devotion*, Radcliffe Biography Series (Reading, MA: A Merloyd Lawrence Book/Addison-Wesley Publishing Company, Inc., 1987), "Preface," xviii.

16. *United States of America v. Eugene V. Debs*, U.S. District Court, Cleveland, Ohio, September 18, 1918. Editor's note: the quotations in this paragraph are all cited in *The Heritage of Debs: The Fight Against War* (Chicago, IL: Socialist Party National Headquarters, 1935), 29.

If we are truly humble we cannot presume that our class, race, citizenship, gender, or education entitle us to any more of the earth's resources than those who have the least. In humility we know that when we have more than what others have it is an injustice that calls for correction; it is a sin that calls for repentance. At the Los Angeles Catholic Worker, where they serve hundreds of people on skid row, before they open their doors to their kitchen, the group of people who are serving gather together to say a prayer attributed to Saint Vincent de Paul. "God, may the poor forgive us this day for the bread that we give them."

Daniel Berrigan is attributed with calling patience a "revolutionary virtue."[17] In this time when national hubris has risen to an obscene level, humility must be counted as an essential revolutionary virtue as well. The Rule of Benedict talks about humility as a ladder that you climb; in Catholic Workers' parlance, we are more likely to talk about a virtue of "downward mobility." These mean the same thing. It is a deliberate, ongoing effort to divest ourselves and to surrender the privileges and wealth that have unjustly accrued to us. I think this might be what Thomas Merton said in his last words. He thought that the monk was a "strange kind of person, a marginal person . . . who withdraws to the margins of society with a view to deepen the fundamental human experience."[18]

Larry Holben wrote a book of theological reflections on the Catholic Worker, which speaks of marginalization as well:

> By setting ourselves outside the sanctioned presumptions and mythologies of the mainstream culture, such marginalization can free us to see that culture and its self-serving distortions with new clarity. As we view the dominant system through the eyes of its victims and losers, we gain a more accurate critical perspective that in itself can provide necessary spiritual detoxification. Standing with

17. Lee Lockwood, "Mother Jones SO93: Still radical after all these years," *Mother Jones* (September/October 1993) online at http://www.motherjones.com/news/hellraiser/1993/09/lockwood.html.

18. *The Asian Journal of Thomas Merton*, edited from his original notebooks by Naomi Burton, Patrick Hart, and James Laughlin (New York: New Directions Publishing Corp., 1973), 305.

the poor in their banishment from the charmed circle of those whose lives are counted important, whose opinions are taken seriously, we can find in our newly discovered helplessness, frustration and even rage, the beginnings of a fresh and more gospel-ready understanding of our world.[19]

Conversation with Meg Funk

Meg: My thanks to the responses to the four elements. Quickly, what we have here is an experience of charisms from where we come. The charism of the Bridgefolk and Mennonites and the question of celibacy is a given. For the majority it is marriage and family as the domestic elemental form. To have a Christ-consciousness of shared love in generativity with family just simply has to be; that is the normal form for the world today. The L'Arche community points us to the particularity to the least and those who actually give us the most because of their singular handicapping conditions that bring us to the elemental. Dorothy, that is a marvelous place; you have to be really fit though. I think the asset of a family setting like that is to recalibrate and to get back to the highest level possible, and then return, and return, and return. That's the essence of an ecclesial gathering. Are we not comforted that our air traffic controller is a member of Sant'Egidio? Again, there is the particularity of in-place, of using the Christian values with like-minded souls. And finally, the Catholic Worker, my favorite story of Dorothy is seeing her with a diaper-sized clothespin in her glasses; she lost a screw obviously. We are all continually challenged by the Catholic Worker and we enable groups to reach out for the social dimension of our communities, especially those who speak for the systems that do need to be changed for the sake of all of us. So, we have hit the elemental there, but there are conversations still to be had.

19. Lawrence Holben, *All the Way to Heaven: A Theological Reflection on Dorothy Day, Peter Maurin and the Catholic Worker* (Rose Hill Books in cooperation with the Los Angeles Catholic Worker, 1997), 37.

*How does one move toward these four ideals? What is the way one is
mentored into them? What is the formation? What is the way this
happens? What are those processes? What are those practices? How
does one really learn them?*

Kathy: I think that one starts from the people who came ahead
of me. I came to L'Arche because I read Henri Nouwen. Maybe lots
of you have heard about L'Arche, too, from him. He was at Daybreak
for ten years. One story he tells is that he helped a core member hang
up his belt every night; for him that was a sacred moment. When I
read that, I was just transformed. So, I took it in. I think it is the
awareness of that and always being open to the awareness of God's
presence. It really comes from the people who have mentored me.
In my case, it was Henri Nouwen. It may be different for you.

Brian: It is very good to have the formation you get out of books
or you get in the classroom, but these things become real as you have
experiences, as you encounter people, and as things happen to you.
I know that one experience I had is that Dorothy Day would always
ask if I had read *The Brothers Karamazov* and *Bread and Wine*; I
would always say, "Yes, I have." But as things would happen in the
course of the living and working, lights go on and I would know what
that meant. The Open Door Community in Atlanta has a wonderful
tradition; before they serve a meal they will often sit down and have
a Bible study together, and then they will open up the doors and serve
the poor. When it is all done, they are all tired, but they sit down and
have their own food and then have a Bible study again, read that
same Scripture and talk about that Scripture in terms of how it is
lived out, whereas earlier it was in the abstract. How did we see this
become real in our work today?

Meg: In the tradition, there are three callings (from Cassian): one
is like Abraham, who was just struck and called in a spiritual intervention; one is out of repentance, where we have failed and we come to
our knees, and we see the light and we want to change our life; the
other is out of imitation: somebody, like Henri Nouwen, or some book
inspires us. The fourth one is already where we are. It is usually right
there in front of your eyes. It is the community we already know and

love; it is our family: our wife/husband, our kids; it is the work we are doing; it is somebody we are talking to already. Usually the grace is so apparent, but we are not recognizing it. Usually it is already something we have done, but we have only done it once. To discern, we do the prophetic thing of what is there and maybe spiritual direction uncovers it, like, "What's going on?" And it is so obvious that we just need the grace to do it and that follows.

Gerald: I would like to tag onto that point: it's there; it's where we are. I have done a lot of reflection as a Benedictine oblate on the proper analogies for me to the vow of stability. I have noticed that our society puts such a premium on keeping us dissatisfied, thinking that real life is happening somewhere else. There is a great phrase in the baptismal formula in the Roman Church: "Do you renounce Satan? Do you renounce the glamour of evil?" I like to tell my students, "If Satan showed up, he wouldn't look as ugly as in all the movies. That would be self-defeating. He wants to look as glamorous as possible." So, there is that constant draw through advertising: find another life situation. Although I haven't made a formal vow of stability that I have to stay geographically where I am in the same way, I have made a vow of marriage and faithfulness to that. But even for people who are not Benedictines, even if I am at a life stage where it is appropriate to be a seeker, I really need to recognize sooner or later that I have to foreclose on some options. If I am a perpetual seeker, I really don't want to find anything, because I am kidding myself. At some point I have to decide to stop looking for that ideal community out there, that ideal life situation, and become mindful of the one I am in. To me that is really pretty basic.

How have our communities become normalized to society, in a positive sense, but also in a negative sense? Where are we going so fast? How do we take the time to listen to ourselves and to each other without so many preoccupations?

Dorothy: One of the very practical concerns we are facing at Holden is the increasing hold of communication technology on

American life in general. This was not an issue for us until recently because we were in this mountain valley where signals could not get through. So, there was only a police radio for emergencies, but now we were told that within the year the satellites will be up, which will permit anyone with a Blackberry to be on the phone or surfing the internet from anywhere in the world. Richard Gaillardetz has a wonderful book arguing that our lives take shape around devices, which order how we live.[20] For Holden and perhaps for other communities, the lure of e-mail and internet surfing and constant stimulation of that sort can really erode efforts at community and pull us away from one another, rather than become embodied in the sense of which God views us and has given us to each other.

Brian: The image of the wheelbarrow is very different from that of a laptop. We really have to think about our life and our work if someone were to make an image of our life in our community. Would they show a picture of a wheelbarrow or of a laptop and fax and printer and all this other stuff?

Meg: That is a wonderful question, which comes back to: What do we want going on in our screen of consciousness as our abiding presence? Seriously, if the afflictions are reduced and are put aside, in other words, if we renounce our inner afflictions and through God's grace they are muted, stilled, we see the beauty; we see each other; we can be this reciprocity in mutuality. But if our consciousness is covered over by our "to do" list, or our greed, or being too busy, which is a form of greed, the culture is ill. The indiscriminate appropriation of the culture was the result of that two-million-dollar study that Lilly did on the religious life in the United States; they said that the biggest obstacle to leading a conscious religious life is indiscriminate cultural assimilation. So, we have to be discriminate and lay it aside. Then we can see if a computer or a cell phone is a skillful means; but if not, we renounce it, because our seeking of God, our experience of God, our knowing God, is our radar, no matter what walk of life we are. We can hear the gentle, subtle promptings of the

---

20. See Richard R. Gaillardetz, *Transforming Our Days: Spirituality, Community and Liturgy in a Technological Culture* (New York: Crossroad, 2000).

Holy Spirit rising up. *Conversatio* means we keep returning, returning; it is an ongoing process. But we need to look at what we want on our radar and plead with God to have mercy on us and give us the skillful means of discernment and the spiritual practices that will lay aside those afflictions.

How do your communities manage differing kinds of availability and different kinds of primary vow structures, for example, for unmarried singles whose focus is on community activities or the married folks whose focus is on their family while living in community?

Craig: Because Sant'Egidio is not a residential community, it makes it a little bit easier. Even in the model of friendship, some people are closer friends and some people are not as close friends. With those who are not as close friends, there is the possibility of moving into a closer friendship circle. So, for our community, it is not a problem. We invite everyone. We are happy to have everyone. We understand that not everyone is in the same place and that not everyone is ready to make the same commitment, but we do have an openness to having everyone or anyone there.

Dorothy: As a Christian wife and mother I think that families have a lot to learn from conversations among monastics about how to help one another be saved, live rightly. When Sr. Meg talked about having a primary community, who are the ones given in the school of forgiveness and mutuality, I think that American families today need to understand one another in that way as well. Insofar as we minister to them, that is an important issue. It might make staying at Holden a long time more difficult, because ultimately it is about sending people out in new primary communities. Holden is not about being a primary community in and of itself as much as it is about sending people out renewed into the primary communities that they will be part of for the rest of their lives, whether monasteries or households.

Brian: Our children have been raised in community; they are grown and away. We have a son living in Buffalo and a daughter who is living at the Catholic Worker House in Chicago and is on the dean's list at Loyola University, and she also made it to the Talon List, the

list the Defense Department has been keeping of people who are serious risks to national security—all before she was twenty-one years
old. We moved when our children were very young from an urban
house of hospitality to a farm, still living in community, but much
smaller and a whole lot more on our terms than what was at the house
of hospitality. One night, when we lived in Davenport, we brought a
child home from the hospital, and somebody broke a window while
we were there. So, we had to find a place, but community was always
very, very essential. A member of our community who lived in another
house and was a former math teacher would do the milking every
evening. When he was waiting for the milk to go through the strainer,
he would do math problems with our kids. They were in public school.
This had a lot more to do with somebody in the community who was
really excited about math, which my wife and I are not; he could pass
this enthusiasm on. For too long I do not think that the nuclear family
is an ideal. The nuclear family is a hideous experiment that was foisted
on us as better cogs in a machine to facilitate capitalism. I appreciate
what was said about the Mennonite versus monastic community: so
much work has not been done on how to do family and community.
This is really something that needs a whole lot more attention. We
are really glad that we did it.

Participant: I am with the Benedictines in Kentucky. As many
of you know, in eastern Kentucky there is mountain-top removal
that is going on; it is very devastating. From a book I read, I wrote
this quote down: "To tear a renewable resource from the ground to
provide a short-term economic gain for the few and long-term environmental destruction for the many is undemocratic, unsustain-
able, and stupid. We are unfortunately a nation that values technology
and wealth much more than we value community. If our species is
to make it through this century, the forces of science and technology
must be tempered by two other forces: ethics and aesthetics."[21] I
would also like to share an opening prayer that fits with the theme:
"Lord, help me to forget everything I think I know; help me to forget
everything I think I know about you; and help me to forget everything
I think I know about others."

21. Erik Reese, "Death of a Mountain: Radical strip mining and leveling of Ap-
palachia," *Harper's Magazine* 310, no. 1859 (April 2005): 60.

"Into the Future" Panel

Mary Ewing Stamps; Timothy Kelly, OSB;
Ephrem Hollermann, OSB; Don Ottenhoff

Presenters on "Into the Future" panel shared their initial learning on the topics taken up in the Monastic Institute and then entertained thoughts on what is on the horizon for monasticism and for Christian communities and its various forms. They fielded questions from each other and the participants. The remarks of each panelist are presented in the order she or he responded.

Mary Ewing Stamps:[1] Recently, when I came into the office, the ceiling was showering down on both the dean's office and mine, which just goes to show the biblical truth: He "sends rain on the righteous and on the unrighteous" (Matt 5:45). It struck me as ironic when I was pondering an event that happened in my own tiny

---

1. Mary Stamps originally comes from Florida. She was educated at Brenau Women's College in Georgia, where she earned a degree in studio art. At Candler School of Theology she earned a master of divinity degree and then a PhD at Emory University in Atlanta. While there she became intrigued by monasticism and monastic life; she came to Saint John's University for a while at the urging of Roberta Bondi and Don Saliers, studied here for a bit in the School of Theology, and then got connected with Upper Room Ministry, an agency of the United Methodist Church. After a few experiments with various people, some from Saint Benedict's Monastery here and support from Saint John's Abbey, in 1999 Mary founded Saint Brigit of Kildare Methodist Monastery. Currently she works as secretary to the dean in the School of Theology, Saint John's University, Collegeville, Minnesota.

monastic house back in the previous spring, when a pipe sprung a leak about two or three days before I found it. In those two to three days before, I had moved all my books and files to the closet in front of where that pipe was. So, by the time I found the leak, over twenty years of notes, lectures, and sermons were pretty much oatmeal. What I learned is: loss is often not as bad as the anticipation of loss. A couple of community members came over to help me clean things up and throw an awful lot of things out, as well as laughing with me about it. The fact is that when it comes to all of that that was represented in those papers in that mush, the details were lost; they were gone and that is fine. But the history and formation that went into collecting those thoughts is still here. So, one thing I have been hearing during this Monastic Institute is that "the times they are 'a'changing.'" The loss is not so bad, because there are an awful lot of gains, and the history they represent is still in there. So, one of the challenges for us in our present and in our future is: How do we think in new ways?

For example, Brother Peregrine referred to a Lutheran pastor who has worked for forty years in trying to establish a monastery out of his tradition and failed. However, here is the challenge: to think a new thought that he has been at it *forty years*. If this Lutheran pastor's goal was to establish a monastery and build up his numbers and his mission and his people, he is on the path to failure. But if his goal was to truly seek God, what are we going to say of him then? And not only that, in the history of that place he took it over from another Lutheran pastor, who around 1948 had tried to do the same thing; so, actually he is the second generation in an almost sixty-year continuous history. So, we need to be urged on to think about things in new ways, as our new monastics encourage us to do.

Often it is a good thing to engage that other sense, because in the back of our minds might be the idea that if we are successful in serving God, it is going to look like Saint John's Abbey or Saint Benedict's Monastery. It is not what that Lutheran pastor is doing. As a trend for the future we will need to accept the gifts that God gives us now and carry them as gifts, not burdens, and to be joyful in the changes that Abbot Notker says are signs of life.

Timothy Kelly, OSB:[2] This topic of old communities and new communities really has a hold on me. A few years ago when Saint John's Abbey had our General Chapter, the education part of that chapter had to do with intentional communities and alternative communities. Prior to the General Chapter, fifteen people were invited to come to Saint John's and have a consultation on the very idea of these kinds of communities, and twelve said "yes," which absolutely amazed me because people were very enthusiastic about the subject matter.

When I think about ideas of new communities in particular, and my contacts with a good number of them, it struck me that what I have to do is go back to the Rule of Saint Benedict and into the life of Benedict to figure out how he did what he did, because he started a new community. He had a model of monastic life that he presented to us. Out of that model of the community, found particularly in the first seven chapters of his Rule, he was dependent on something that went before him.

So, looking at the model of monastic life that he leaves us suggests three things to us. First, as a witness to prior tradition, the Rule of Benedict has much to offer new communities even today. Second, as an example of listening, monastic communities still listen to the experience of others "who cherish Christ above all" (RB 72.11). Third, the younger communities of our day have much to offer traditional communities. Benedict, after all, took the prior Rule of the Master, adopted it, and adapted it to a new vision of monastic life.

First, ancient monastic wisdom has much to say and teach to those who would seek ways of living the monastic tradition today. Of very great importance is to recognize that this monastic tradition is

2. Abbot Timothy Kelly, OSB, made his initial commitment to Benedictine life in 1955 and was ordained to the priesthood in 1961. Among other positions over his career, he has taught English and theology, been chaplain to Benedictine women monastics, director of novices, and rector of Saint John's Seminary. He worked coincidentally with the Methodist Upper Room Ministry to explore monastic possibilities within the Methodist Church, where he connected with Mary Stamps. He continues to serve on the Catholic China Bureau. In 1992 he was elected the ninth abbot of Saint John's Abbey, in which capacity he served until 2000. In 2003 he was elected President of the American Cassinese Congregation of Benedictine Monasteries.

a *living* tradition. Secondly, new endeavors in our day to adapt wisely the principles of the living monastic tradition have much to teach traditional monastic communities. These older communities are quite capable of circling the wagons to protect that with which they are comfortable, which, in turn, can stifle growth and silence the Spirit. If such communities would continue to live and to be *wisdom* communities, they must listen to what the Spirit is saying to the churches. The one who has ears to hear must so listen (cf. Matt 13:9).

Some time ago "The Word from Rome" by John Allen, which is found on the internet, had an interesting couple of paragraphs. After speaking about some of the challenges the church faces, Allen states:

> In other words, the central challenge for world Catholicism at the moment is not decline, but growth, and making sense of the new interactions between faith and culture this growth is generating.
>
> "Rearranging deck chairs on the Titanic" has passed into the cultural idiom as a synonym for blithe indifference to an underlying crisis. I would suggest that much conversation in Western Catholicism these days is more akin to arguing over which buggy whips are best, while ignoring the emergence of the car; that is, a completely new world is taking shape, one destined to render many of this era's debates obsolete.
>
> What I have called the "upside down church" of the future, one driven increasingly by the experience and priorities of the South, is likely to take scant interest in matters that have set the Catholic agenda in the West for more than a century, such as the balance of power between Rome and the bishops, or debates over various questions of doctrine. Instead, it will be the "cash value" of Catholicism in the confrontation with poverty, disease, corruption, war and cultural conflict that will increasingly be on the minds of most Catholics on the planet.
>
> So why is the West still arguing over buggy whips?[3]

The reason for quoting that is simply because we have to be aware of doing the same thing in our traditional monastic communities.

3. John L. Allen Jr., "The Expansion of Catholicism in the South," *National Catholic Reporter-NCR Online.org* 5, no. 40 (June 16, 2006); http://nationalcatholicreporter .org/word/word061606.htm.

Saint Benedict lived in a time with some similar characteristics to our own time. His solution monastically was to establish a society where God could be sought in company with others committed to the same way of life. He proclaimed Christ as the leader of the community, as the *pater familias*, and the abbot as the chief steward who guided his fellow servants. Rank, generally speaking, depended on who got in line first when entering the monastery. Slave or free made no difference.

The monastery was the place to experience Christ in the abbot, in the guest, in the elderly and infirm, in fact in each other and in everyone. Benedict gave a Rule designed to give the experience of church as Christ and Christ as church—because we are the Body of Christ and identify with each other because we see each other in Christ.

What Benedictine monasticism can offer today is the dual value of identifying ourselves as Christ and of being joined together in church or Body of Christ. He recognized and legislated a spirituality of presence in Christ with the minimum of external organization—whatever was needed to keep any society together.

Because Benedict also recognized the monastery as part of the church and not apart from it, he implicitly establishes the monastic community as a sort of sacrament of what the whole church is. He recognizes the value of each person, but calls each person to responsibility for the whole community. The community together is a sacrament for the church and for the neighborhood, recognized especially by its hospitality to guests.

Now let us address the future. Cardinal Oscar Andrés Rodriguez de Maradiaga, archbishop of Tegucigalpa, Honduras, speaking of the contemporary condition of the church, said: "It is sad to me to see how mission has been neglected in favor of maintenance when what we need above all is mission."[4] This would simply be a cliché except that the communities of our congregations and federations

4. Austen Ivereigh, "The high flyer from Honduras" [Interview of Cardinal-Archbishop Oscar Andrés Rodriguez de Maradiaga, archbishop of Tegucigalpa, Honduras], *The Tablet* (8 November 2003), 5.

recognize the precarious condition of many if not all of us. We do not like to use the word "precarious," but it is probably the reality that is haunting all of us in varying degrees.

At the 2002 Chapter of the Cistercians of the Strict Observance (OCSO), this issue of precariousness was squarely faced. An ad hoc commission was established whose task was to gather reports from committees that had been named and to synthesize the findings. The result is a document entitled: "Vision of the Order, 2002." The opening line of the report said: "Our great surprise was to find that nearly all the communities are in a precarious situation."[5]

Instead of lamenting this fact, they wanted to know: "What can enable us to profit from our precariousness? . . .Why do we want to survive?"[6] After listing four reasons for continued existence, they say this:

> Ultimately, our concern is not with the survival of the Order but with the building up of the Church of Christ. Insofar as we are convinced that our life is a genuine charism that enables men and women to grow in communion in Christ, we have the mission of living it to the full and thereby transmitting it to others, to the next generation and generations. Vocation and mission coincide. . . . We are discovering that sometimes our charism is life-giving not so much in the continuance of life within a particular community, but rather in other communities, countries and forms of ecclesial life. We thus transform our experiences of diminishment and precariousness in union with Christ, giving our lives that others might live.[7]

This statement of the cardinal-archbishop of Tegucigalpa is impressive because he is addressing an issue of which we must all be aware. Individual communities are facing problems similar to those addressed by the Cistercians. Most of our communities have been in existence many decades, and have developed ministries that have

---

5. "Vision of the Order 2002," findings of the Mixed General Meeting held at the Generalate of the Brothers of Christian Schools, Via Aurelia 476, Rome, as found on the following web site: http://www.ocso.org/docfinmgm-en.htm.

6. Ibid.

7. Ibid.

contributed to the life of the church in valuable ways. We often find ourselves with inherited responsibilities and fewer monastics to support them with their labors. People have become dependent on us and we do not want to pull back and disappoint them, so we work our membership even harder. So, frequently our focus is on maintaining what we have, rather than discovering other ways to listen to and apply what God may be calling us to in terms of mission.

The world has changed and, while holding to the essentials of our monastic life, we are called upon *not* to circle the wagons and protect what gives us security, but to be open to ways God may be calling us today. This is not a call to give up what we are doing in our apostolates and missions, but to be alert as to how we can use our talents most effectively in helping people to seek God as we profess to do.

Ephrem Hollermann, OSB:[8] I have found this to be a daunting task. For one who has to ponder, and ponder again for weeks and months, this panel response to the experiences of this week's Monastic Institute is a stretch.

Preliminary Remarks

I want first to acknowledge the committee for putting together a program for this Institute that attracted this remarkable group of people. The rich and diverse notions of monasticism and communal seeking reflected in this year's Institute have resulted in a kind of "new Pentecost" experience for me. At times, while interacting with people here, I've felt like a new language of monasticism is being born in our time. At first blush some aspects of the conversation have felt something like a foreign language to my ears and heart,

8. Sister Ephrem Hollermann, OSB, earned a BA at the College of Saint Benedict in elementary education and social science, an MA in theology from Saint John's, and a PhD in historical theology from Marquette, where she did a dissertation on American Benedictine women in the nineteenth century. Since then she has taught junior high, high school, and college. She has served as a novice director, director of initial formation, and prioress of Saint Benedict's Monastery from 1995 to 2005. In that capacity, she had the opportunity to observe and interact with dozens of other communities, especially women's communities and their way of life.

which have been trained in a pretty classical and mainstream brand of Benedictine monasticism within the Roman Catholic tradition. But as the week wore on and I listened more deeply, I have come to know in my heart of hearts that, diverse as we are in this room, we do understand one another at a very deep level, though we may use different "languages." At the level of our "one heart, one soul" we desire, to use Abbot Notker's words, "to live with God in a Benedictine way."

Abbot Primate Notker Wolf mentioned Abbot Boniface Wimmer as the founder of the Bavarian tradition of Benedictine monasticism on North American soil. He did not, however, mention Mother Benedicta Riepp, as the foundress of that same tradition among women, a mere eleven years after Boniface Wimmer arrived here. Given the overall theme of this week—"one heart, one soul," I cannot go on without quoting what I find to be the most poignant and important words in Mother Benedicta Riepp's extant correspondence. (By the way, we have only fourteen extant letters of Mother Benedicta Riepp, but two thousand—plus letters of Abbot Boniface Wimmer. They are preserved in the archives of Saint Vincent Archabbey in Latrobe, Pennsylvania.)

Three years before her death here in Saint Cloud, Minnesota, Mother Benedicta, writing to Cardinal Barnabo in Rome, put into words the only goal worth striving for in our Benedictine way of life:

> It would be my consolation and joy if our new foundations in America, of which there are four at present, were to remain united, . . . so that one spirit and one life could be preserved in all the hearts of the Sisters. I believe that in America especially the unity of the order, particularly in what pertains to the Holy Rule and the statutes, could by a common bonding together more securely and easily guaranteed, fostered and preserved than one way of life and one love would obtain among all.[9]

9. As translated by Incarnata Girgen, OSB, *Behind the Beginnings: Benedictine Women in America* (St. Paul, MN: North Central Publishing Company for Saint Benedict's Convent, Saint Joseph, Minnesota, 1981), 136–37.

These words were written on January 4, 1859, thirteen years after her first profession at Saint Walberg Abbey, in Eichstätt, Bavaria, less than a year after she arrived in North America, and three years before her death at age thirty-six. "One way of life, one love." "One heart, one soul: many communities."

For more than twenty years, I have been trying to gather and put together the pieces of the founding story of Benedictine women in North America. I would much rather be speaking about that remarkable nineteenth-century story today than to be responding to the question of "into the future." There is no clear path "into the future." But I do believe that this Institute's unusual experience has given us some glimpses of what may lie ahead, and certainly has raised important questions and issues for continuing the dialogue. These questions and issues beg our earnest prayer for the guidance of the Holy Spirit of God as we move into the future.

Among the many things that have tugged at my heart this week, I will share just two. These deal specifically with our experience as North American Benedictine women at this time in our history. (I look over this room of participants and muse about who is the visible majority here. Women religious just keep showing up!)

I want to invite those of you who are not women, who are not North American, who are not Roman Catholic, who are not professed monastics in the formal sense, into our experience. I invite you into this pondering because I believe you have a vantage point of understanding, insight, and perspective that we cannot have from inside our own experience.

Collective Spiritual Maturity and Wisdom

My first "into the future" reflection is inspired by what I heard from Columba Stewart, Notker Wolf, Christine Pohl, Margaret Malone, Meg Funk, and the breakout sessions on new communities.

Abbot Primate Notker noted that there has been an increase of about five hundred Benedictine women globally since the year 2000. What he did not say is that historically the largest Benedictine communities of women in the world have been in North America. Further, he did not point out that the increase in global membership today is largely due to burgeoning memberships in the African and Asian women's communities. Today there are approximately three thousand Benedictine women in North America. In 1975, thirty years ago, there were approximately six thousand four hundred of us. The median age in our communities across the country today is somewhere in the decade of the seventies, closing in on eighty in some communities. Over the past one hundred fifty years, we have helped to educate an immigrant Catholic Church, we have cared for the sick, and we have served in roles too numerous to count. We have "hung in there"; we have "shown up"; we have endured enormous change at the church's bidding; we have been misunderstood; and we have clung fiercely to the vision of Vatican Council II with its focus on reform, renewal, and inclusion.

When Abbot Primate Notker spoke of monastic challenges and hopes and signs of life in our times, he used the image of a people on a journey, suggesting that we at the dawn of the twenty-first century are in the desert of a very changed world. Columba Stewart suggested that we are in a time of transition, not unlike that of the fourth to the seventh centuries, when Benedictine monasticism came to birth in the West.

These images and insights have given me pause to consider that we North American Benedictine women today are, indeed, listening and straining to hear the new call of the desert. It might be well for us to embrace in these times a kind of "remnant spirituality" that is pregnant with joyful waiting in communities of hope and love—that image that was so beautifully described by Margaret Malone and in other words by Christine Pohl. To her surprise, our biblical fore-mother, Sarah, found herself pregnant in an advanced age and laughed. Recall that God has done wonderful things with remnant peoples in Judeo-Christian history.

Let us not forget that North American Benedictine women were born out of a remnant German community. Thirteen elderly women survived the Napoleonic secularization of their monastery in Eich-stätt in 1806, and were ready to begin anew in 1835 when their mon-astery was restored. By the time Mother Benedicta Riepp made her first profession ten years later in that monastery, all thirteen members of the old community had died, and the "new wave" of members was thrust into the future. There is also a Swiss tradition of Benedictine women in North America stemming from Sarnen and Mechtal in Switzerland later in the nineteenth century, and their stories are equally compelling.

I have pondered much about where our communities are at this time in history. We are often tempted to describe ourselves as "aging communities," as if that is the only identity we now have. I would rather have us think of ourselves as communities having "come of age." At no other time in our one-hundred-fifty-year history in North America have we been at this point of collective spiritual maturity and wisdom that can only come with age and experience. In these times God is leading us at so many levels of "letting go" in this desert time of our history. We are experiencing numerous deaths accompanied by an enormous sense of loss of our mentors and friends. We have been letting go of the esteem and appreciation we once enjoyed at the height of our institutional commitments. We are needing to let go of our time-honored buildings, and in some cases are downsizing and relocating in other places. Letting go of the way we were is becoming a way of life for us.

I have come to feel enormously blessed to be living in this, our era of collective spiritual maturity and wisdom. God is leading us ever more deeply to desire the one thing necessary—the search for God alone, in the paradox of a more focused and contemplative prayer life on the one hand, and a more expansive and inclusive presence in and love of the world, on the other hand. Being with so many new and varied Benedictine and monastic seekers compels me, against this backdrop, to ask: What can you take from us and our one-hundred-fifty-year history in North America, and what can we give away from who we are at this time in our history that will empower you to birth new forms of Christian and Benedictine communities for the coming age of monastic seeking?

To Dream of Communities of Inclusion

My second "into the future" reflection is briefer and in some ways feels like the "elephant in the room." It is a reflection based on words from Father Kevin Seasoltz, Christine Pohl, and Margaret Malone, and from the moments of sadness I experienced after this Institute's session on the Eucharist. It is about some key formative elements of community—the table of thanksgiving and inclusion (so eloquently described by Margaret Malone), the celebration of Eucharist (with such theological richness presented by Kevin Seasoltz), and truth telling (one of the authentic marks of hospitable communities described by Christine Pohl).

Clearly, Eucharist within the monastic community is central to its life of worship, prayer, and brotherly/sisterly love. Ponder with me for a moment the differing experience celebrating the Eucharist in men's and women's monastic communities. In a men's community, one from among them is privileged to come forward to lead the community in eucharistic celebration—to bring to the altar *all* the life that has been lived with his brothers in the intimacy of daily community life: the struggles, the joys, the good times, the bad times, the conflicts, the forgivenesses, all of it.

When a women's community gathers for Eucharist, a relative stranger comes into their midst who has not lived it all with them in the more intimate circle of their community life. I have often wondered what it would be like for us if a member of my own community, of my own gender, could lead us at the altar of eucharistic celebration, having lived the messiness and blessedness of our communal striving with us.

I speak of this here from the point of view of our single-gendered monastic communities in the Roman Catholic tradition, but I should like all of us to ponder the position of women in reference to eucharistic leadership in authentic Christian communities. Can we dream of authentic community at all as long as women continue to be marginalized at many levels in our Christian churches and communities? Are the communities we have dreamed about this week possible at all when forms of exclusion exist at the eucharistic table? This is not simply an item of feminist agenda about the ordination of women.

These questions are about the need to eliminate the sin of exclusion at the Table.

Can we dare to dream that our monastic brothers and other male ministers of the Eucharist in our churches will do everything in their power and from their position of privilege in the culture and in the church to bring about change with regard to the status of women and other powerless ones in our Christian churches? If, indeed, there is nothing that can be done about this, then I have to wonder if the kingdom of God can truly come "on this earth as it is in heaven."

Don Ottenhoff:[10] I will share with you a little piece of sightseeing advice: never take a guided tour of a cathedral until you have given yourself plenty of time to encounter the reality and significance of the whole. Otherwise a guide, or a guidebook, will yammer on about detail after detail and you may not allow yourself the opportunity to hear the stunning harmonics of the very space that surrounds you.

That personal advice haunts me; I do not want any details I may highlight to detract from the remarkable reality of the *whole*: religious communities of very different sorts, representing different religious traditions, and from various parts of the globe, have come together to compare notes and learn from one another. What is more, participants sense that the experience and wisdom of the Benedictine tradition holds particular relevance to broad religious and cultural issues that impinge upon all of us. The feature of *this* institute that seems to bear the most significance for the future is simply that it has happened, in *this* place, with *these* people, and with *this* theme, "One Heart, One Soul: Many Communities." It will be even more important for the future that the conversations begun here continue. Perhaps in the future we can have a manifesto: "Benedictines of the world unite."

Having said that, two details have particular bearing on the future development of Christian religious communities and how we learn from one another.

10. Don Ottenhoff, who is a native of Chicago, did his undergraduate work at Calvin College in Michigan, master of divinity degree at McCormick Theological Seminary, and worked on his PhD at the University of Chicago. Don is an ordained minister in the Presbyterian Church USA, and worked at the *Christian Century* from 1991 until 2004, serving as senior editor for six years. Since 2004 he is the director of the Collegeville Institute for Ecumenical and Cultural Research.

First, it has become clear that intergenerational issues are not simply concerns we face within communities, but are also factors among communities. As the Abbot Primate pointed out, long-established Benedictine communities are struggling with issues of sustainability, and every member of this panel has mentioned this. Other communities, as Jonathan Wilson-Hartgrove reminded us, are working through the challenges of infancy, and still others are somewhere in between.

One concern among others is that generation gaps *among* communities may hinder communication *between* them. For example, the Abbot Primate listed a number of challenges Benedictine communities face, and said, "Give us time" to discover and implement new answers to new problems. But I wrote in my notes, "You don't have the time. People are knocking on your door for guidance *now*."

Let me state my concern in a slightly different way. It seems to be the case—from the resonance of Alasdair MacIntyre's appeal to a new Saint Benedict,[11] to the growth of oblate programs, to the number of people at this very Institute—that the Benedictine tradition has moved into a moment of distinct historical opportunity—as the New Testament would say, it is *en kairo*—it is a Kairos moment for Benedictines. Hopefully the very real internal challenges of Benedictine communities do not hinder them from providing the kind of insight and creative leadership that is expected of them now and in the future.

Second, this gathering has convinced me that Benedictine communities should serve in the future as principal sites for the continuing work of ecumenism. In the last century, ecumenists gathered in places that looked like corporate headquarters. As Abbot John and others observe, Benedictine life, which is based on a Rule that predates major divisions within Christianity, provides a unique setting of prayer and worship, which should be at the heart of all ecumenical work.

---

11. Alasdair MacIntyre, *After Virtue: A Study in Moral Theory*, 3rd ed. (Notre Dame, IN: University of Notre Dame Press, 2006), 263.

Obviously, the Benedictine's journey into Rome poses ecumenical challenges, but the four "enduring essentials of Benedictine life" that Meg Funk detailed—listening, community, humility, and hospitality—should mark all ecumenical encounters. When these essentials are shared to the extent possible, and where not fully shared, fully respected, then the grace of full communion will surely follow. That is a Benedictine and ecumenical future I long for.

Summative Probings
for the Movement of Monasticism "Into the Future"

Mary Forman, OSB

Several values emerged from the last dialogue among participants, panelists, and speakers concerning the future of monasticism, both traditional Benedictine forms and the new emerging forms of intentional communities, new monasticism groups, and oblates. Hopefully, the following impressions will articulate "the poignancy of the dialogue"[1] and provide soundings of hope for the future development of Christian communal life.

Mutual Hospitality

A member of Bridgefolk expressed appreciation for a Benedictine community opening its doors and hearts to dialogue between Mennonites and Catholics, which has resulted in an unaccountable exchange of gifts and yet-to-be-realized bases for understanding communal life. Benedictine communities were invited and requested to reach out in loving hospitality to their Protestant neighbors and to share their wisdom. It may be as simple as inviting nearby faith

---

1. Several phrases have been borrowed from the dialogue at the final session of the Institute, but the name of the person who said it is unknown.

communities to a meal and sharing or the adoption of a new community into a mutual mentoring of each other through the exchange of collective wisdom, providing retreats, and sharing of stories and experiences of living communal life. In the process, the real fears and prejudices of individuals and collective bodies will need to be addressed with honesty and care.

As each denomination faces the inevitable changes that its polity addresses, matters like the ordination of women and the sexual orientation of its ministerial leadership, a great sensitivity will be needed to hold the ecumenical dialogue on controversial issues and the differing points of view in creative tension with the desire to seek what is of God. At the heart of the kind of hospitality required to be led by the Spirit into these dialogues is the biblical teaching that each person, male and female, is made in the image and likeness of God, and thus to be respected as such.

Formation

A number of voices expressed the desire for dialogue around formation: What does it take to form new folks who come to community? How are issues of obedience, authority, and discipline addressed in the community? How does the community deal with dying and the preparations for death with profound respect for the dignity of individuals and of the community?

There is a call for parallel conversations between communities of faith of the baptized in parishes with communities of faith that live intentional communal lives: how might parishes and monastic communities mutually enrich, support, and deepen one another's common life? In addition, how might the "very intense laboratory for Christian living," which the intentional community strives to be, feed the rest of the community in its mission and ministry to the wider world?

Formation itself entails ongoing lifelong learning to live the Gospel life and remembering the benefits and graces that come from reformation in all its varied nuances and historical realities. Many traditional communities have taken up the task of formation of oblates and associate members to carry Benedictine spirituality out into the world through the daily lives of committed men and women. Newer forms of community are seeking ways to form their members for the long haul despite disappointment in expectations, real friction that inevitably arises, and the pain of suffering that must be given over to healing.

There is a collective wisdom from a form of monastic life that has existed in its various incarnations for over fifteen hundred years that is both gift and challenge to be shared: what has been learned from the experience of communal life that can serve as guide and object lessons for others? At the same time, communities like the Quakers have their own processes of discernment, which can bear witness to values often called monastic, but are nonetheless those of the Gospel like simplicity, peace, harmony, integrity, community, and equality. Christian traditions seek that which is of God in each person, so, how do we mutually enrich each other's paths?

Issues for Communities of the Future

One of the issues for fruitful dialogue between traditional monastics and married members of faith communities is the intersection of celibacy and marriage, particularly as the dynamics of leadership, obedience, and authority are played out in community. A related issue is that of how the various generations in monastic communities have or have not dealt with sexuality, sexual orientation, and generativity. Because of the unease regarding celibacy in American culture today, conversations about sexuality and celibacy by married people and monastics could bring an intelligibility to our world for how to live as sexual beings. In addition, monastics and families could grow in a realistic, rather than romanticized, understanding of one another's commitment.

A matter of concern, certainly for monastics and quite possibly other kinds of community members, is that of "right-sizing," that is, how to face the diminishments of dying and downsizing communities without losing the creative energy for moving forward with a mission into the future.

There is also the challenge of the corrosive influence that marginalized people can have in a community and how to combat the attitudes of the competitive individualities and self-centered culture in which we live, so that members do not create "comfortable ministerial niches" for themselves or end up losing their vocation because they consistently refuse to enter into the daily life of the community. In other words, "how responsible are we for those whom we have initiated into our communities?"

Prophetic Challenges

This kind of question calls us to face, as Jesus did, the inability to be a prophet to one's own community. However, "no one is ever in full possession of the prophetic spirit at one time nor long-term." So, we are called to be vigilant: to hear the voices of the Spirit in our midst—"from the left to the right, the old or the young" or the Northern vis-à-vis the Southern Hemisphere. These voices may challenge our previous understandings, and this challenge will certainly mean facing the significant differences that exist among community members. It will also mean experiencing "the pleasure of not knowing," that is, not having a crystal ball about the future but needing to trust that we are being led.

Here history can serve to teach us. One way is that of "remnant spirituality," that is, the biblical experience of being reduced in number and awaiting the birthing, letting go, and waiting process, of which the prophets spoke. God is the one who brings new life out of a remnant people; the people keep vigilant by being faithful to God, waiting on God to bring something new. This kind of "waiting is a very pregnant thing, not passive; it is a stance of listening for the Spirit's guidance and direction in the next step that needs to be taken."

At the same time that history teaches us to wait and let things happen, it also teaches that there are other times where we make something happen, as a kind of "active intervention in history," in which people feel called to act on behalf of others out of a sense of being missioned as disciples of Christ. The very hardness, difficulty, and beauty of communal life can be a compelling witness to a world that is hungry to see people living together truthfully in the context of love and hospitality.

Signs of Hope

One presenter shared her three signs of hope from the conversations of the Institute: (1) the very meeting together and conversing about community in its many rich and diverse dimensions; (2) the new people whose lives are so vital and vibrant, who despite not knowing what lies ahead are willing to live in community; and (3) the older members whose wisdom sustains the community and whose fidelity witnesses to the God-who-is-with-us on the journey.

Conclusion

As Meg Funk stated, "the real purpose of dialogue is the process of the dialogue itself," that is, being present to one another, learning to appreciate differences, being able to discover the Christ in each other, and being able to call forth the best from each other, so together we offer something vital to the world. The dialogue between professed monastics and new monastics of various forms was indeed rich with moments of the awareness of "one heart and one soul," as also the realization that there are enough real differences and challenges for future conversations.

Index

215

Scriptural References

Rule of Benedict References